LANGUAGE

of the

Piano

BY

DOROTHY PRIESING

LIBBIE TECKLIN

A

WORK BOOK

IN THEORY AND KEYBOARD

HARMONY

CARL FISCHER®

O4131

ISBN 978-1-4911-0289-8

FOREWORD

LANGUAGE OF THE PIANO is a workbook with a two-fold purpose:
1. To develop keyboard and analytic skills.
2. To apply these skills to the performance of piano music.

The book may be used in private and class instruction, in secondary piano, and in theory and keyboard harmony classes.

The selection of material includes examples from early keyboard literature to music of the present day. A bibliography has been added to stimulate further study and exploration.

This book is an outgrowth of our private and class instruction given in the Preparatory Division of the Juilliard School of Music, New York City.

We wish to thank Frances Mann, Director of the Preparatory Division of the Juilliard School of Music, for her interest and encouragement.

Libbie Teuklin
Dorothy Priesing

June 23, 1959

TABLE OF CONTENTS

PART IV. CADENCES AND HARMONIZATIONS

PART V. FORM

PART I
Scale Structures

THE MAJOR SCALE

The MAJOR SCALE is one of the most common scale-structures. All MAJOR SCALES must have the same pattern, (arrangement of whole and half-steps).

The MAJOR SCALE is made up of two tetrachords. Each tetrachord consists of two whole-steps and a half-step. A whole-step lies between the tetrachords. The second tetrachord of each scale becomes the first tetrachord of the new scale in the circle of keys.

NOTE: the half-steps between 3-4 and 7-8, making the MAJOR SCALE pattern 12345678.

TERMS TO KNOW:

A *Half-step* on the piano is the distance from one key to the very next key. Ex.: C-Db or E-F.
A *Whole-step* on the piano contains two half-steps. Ex: C-D or E-F♯.
The term *Key* means tone-family grouped around the Key note (1st scale-step). Ex: Key of Eb Major.
The term *Key-signature* means the sharps or flats placed immediately after the clef sign. These accidentals indicate in what Key the music is written. Ex: the Key-signature of two sharps usually means the Key of D Major.
Enharmonic means two spellings of the same sound: C♯ and Db.

Study the CIRCLE OF MAJOR KEYS and KEY SIGNATURES given below.

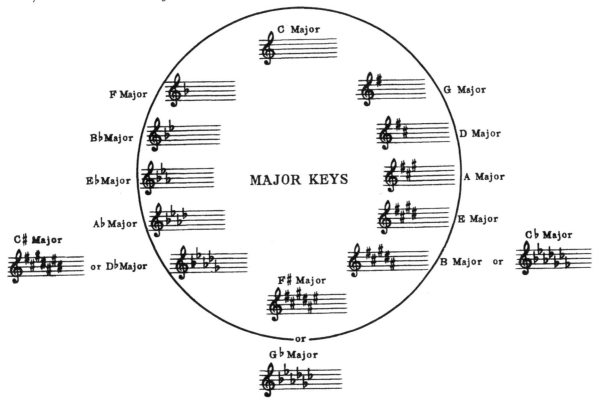

LESSON 1
The Major Scale—C Major

Write in 𝄞 and 𝄢 : the C MAJOR SCALE, one octave ascending.
Mark half-steps. Play until familiar.

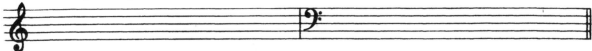

Study Ex. 1.   Name and write key.   Circle the MAJOR SCALE.   Play:

Key: ☐

Allegro Moderato

PASTORALE DANCE
Ludwig van Beethoven

LESSON 2
The Major Scale—G Major

Write in 𝄞 and 𝄢 : the G MAJOR SCALE, with KEY SIGNATURE, one octave, ascending.
Mark half-steps.   Play until familiar.

Study Ex. 2.   Name and write key.   Circle the MAJOR SCALES.   Play:

Key: ☐

Allegro Moderato

INVENTION AND LITTLE FUGUE
J. P. Kirnberger

LESSON 3
The Major Scale—F Major

Write in 𝄞 and 𝄢 : the F MAJOR SCALE with key signature, one octave, ascending.
Mark half-steps.   Play until familiar.

Study Ex. 3.   Name and write key.   Circle the MAJOR SCALE.   Play:

Key: ☐

Allegretto

WALTZ IN F
Ludwig van Beethoven

2

N3167

LESSON 4
The Major Scale—D Major

Write in 𝄞 and 𝄢 : the D MAJOR SCALE, with key signature, one octave, ascending.
Mark half-steps. Play until familiar.

Study Ex. 4. Name and write key. Circle the MAJOR SCALE. Play:

Key: ☐ **Allegro non troppo**

ALLEMANDE
Maurice Greene

f non legato

LESSON 5
The Major Scale—B Flat Major

Write in 𝄞 and 𝄢 the B♭ MAJOR SCALE with key signature, one octave, ascending.
Mark half-steps. Play until familiar.

Study Ex. 5. Name and write key. Circle the MAJOR SCALE. Play:

Key: ☐

GERMAN DANCE #4
Franz J. Haydn

Moderato

mf

LESSON 6
Review of Major Scales

Piano music is full of scale-line. At times the complete scale in one or more octaves is used; at times only *part* of it. Study the examples below. Find all MAJOR SCALES, *complete* or in *part*. Name them. Play:

Key: ☐ **Allegro vivace**

TEASING
Bela Bartok

mf

Permission for reprint granted by G. Schirmer Inc., New York, N. Y., copyright owner.

3

ALLEGRO FROM LITTLE SUITE #3
Johann W. Hassler

WORK SHEET

On the staves below, write with key signatures the given MAJOR SCALES, one octave ascending. Mark half-steps. Play until familiar.

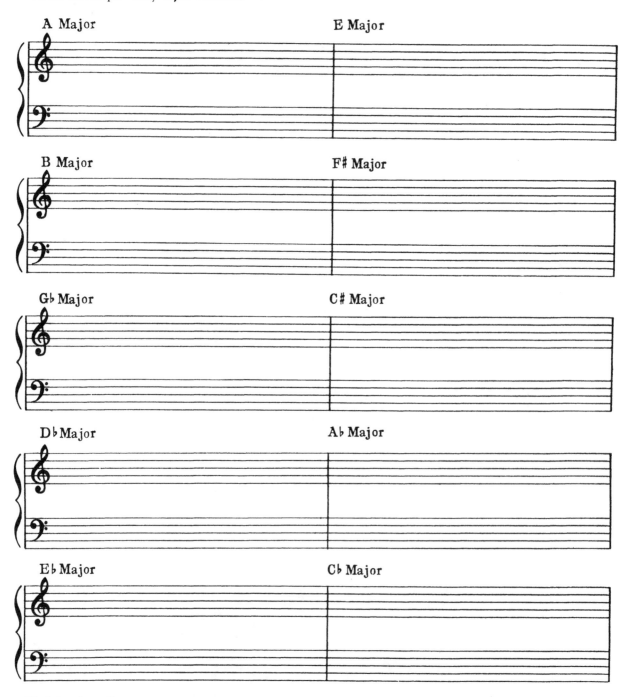

A Major

E Major

B Major

F♯ Major

G♭ Major

C♯ Major

D♭ Major

A♭ Major

E♭ Major

C♭ Major

Find in piano literature examples of MAJOR SCALES.

LESSON 7
The Minor Scales—Tonic Minor

The MINOR SCALE beginning on the same keynote as a MAJOR SCALE is called its TONIC (PARALLEL) MINOR. TONIC MINORS occur in three forms, Natural, Harmonic and Melodic.

To change a MAJOR SCALE to NATURAL form, lower 3, 6, 7 one half-step.
To change a MAJOR SCALE to HARMONIC form, lower 3 and 6 one half-step.
To change a MAJOR SCALE to MELODIC form, lower 3 ascending and 7, 6, 3 descending, one half-step.

WORK SHEET

On the staves below, write the MAJOR and TONIC (PARALLEL) MINOR scales, one octave, ascending. Mark half-steps. Play until familiar.

A Major

D Major

A Minor (Natural)

D Minor (Natural)

G Major

F Major

G Minor (Harmonic)

F Minor (Melodic)

Relative Minor

Observe: the NATURAL MINOR SCALE above has three flats. If the key signature of three flats is used, the minor is said to be the *Relative Minor* of E♭ MAJOR. The relative minor scales begin on the 6th degree of the major scale. Play:

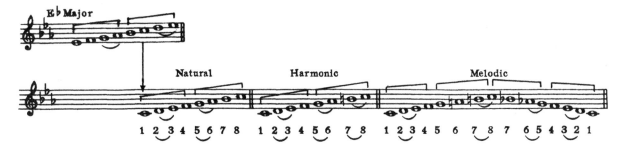

N3167

Study the CIRCLE OF RELATIVE MINOR KEYS AND KEY SIGNATURES given below.

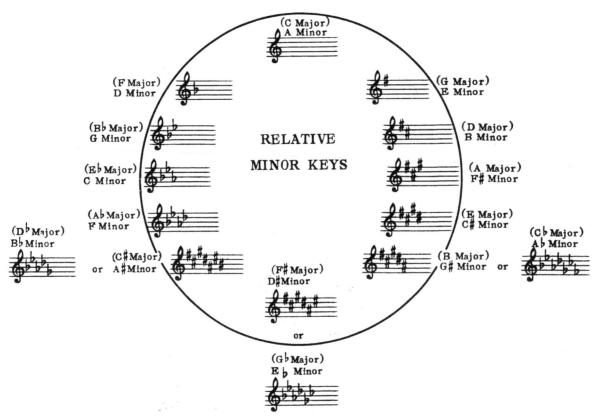

Memorize: The TONIC MINOR has the same keynote as the TONIC MAJOR.
the RELATIVE MINOR has the same key signature as the RELATIVE MAJOR.

WORK SHEET

On the staves below, write the GIVEN MAJOR and RELATIVE MINOR SCALES.
Mark half-steps. Play until familiar.

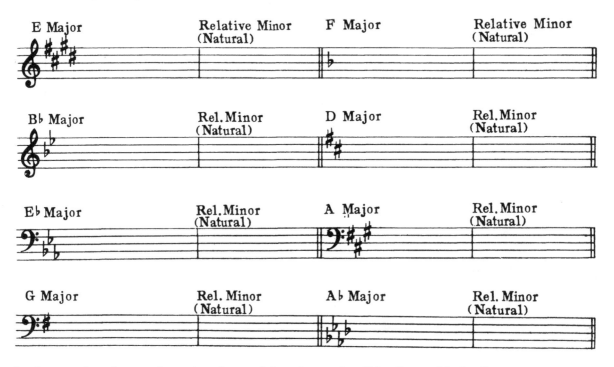

In the next three lessons, the various forms of the minor scale will be discussed in detail.

N3167

LESSON 8
Natural Minor

The NATURAL MINOR is an unaltered scale, using the relative major key signature.
Note: Half-steps between 2-3 and 5-6.

Write in 𝄞 and 𝄢 : the E MINOR SCALE (NATURAL form), with key signature.
Mark half-steps. Play until familiar.

Study Ex. 8 and Ex. 9. Name and write the key of each. Circle the NATURAL MINOR SCALES. Play:

Key: ☐

MAZURKA, OP. 8 #9
V. Rebikov

Key: ☐

A LITTLE SONG
D. Kabalevsky

WORK SHEET

On the staves below, write the following RELATIVE MINOR SCALES (NATURAL form) with key signature, one octave, ascending. Mark the half-steps. Play until familiar.

G Minor   B Minor

F♯ Minor   C♯ Minor

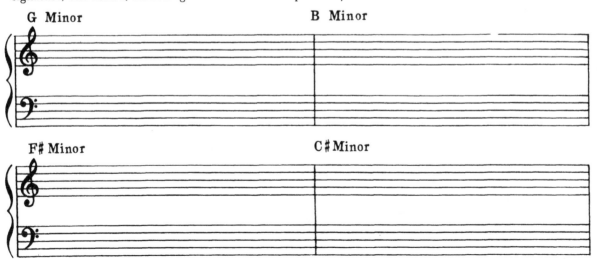

7

G# Minor   Eb Minor

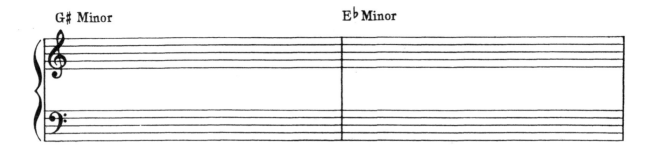

Bb Minor   F Minor

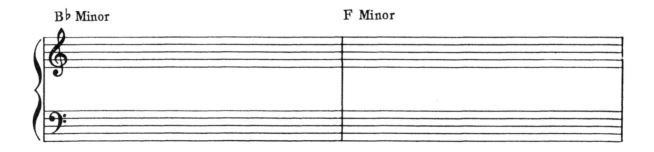

D# Minor   D Minor

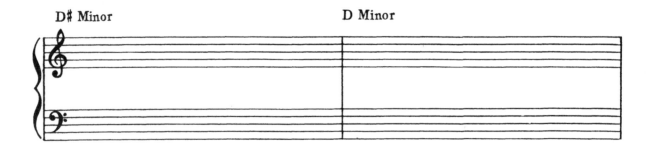

Find in piano literature examples of the NATURAL MINOR SCALE.

LESSON 9
Harmonic Minor

The HARMONIC MINOR is an altered minor with a raised 7th, using the relative major signature.

Note: Half-steps between 2-3, 5-6, and 7-8.

Write in 𝄞 and 𝄢 : the G MINOR SCALE (HARMONIC form) with key signature, one octave, ascending.   Mark the half-steps.   Play until familiar.

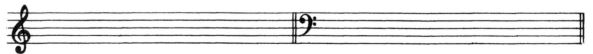

8

N3167

Study Ex. 10 and 11.   Name and write key of each.   Circle the HARMONIC MINOR SCALES.   Play.

Key: ☐

SONATE #11
D. Cimarosa

Key: ☐

PUPPET'S COMPLAINT
Cesar Franck

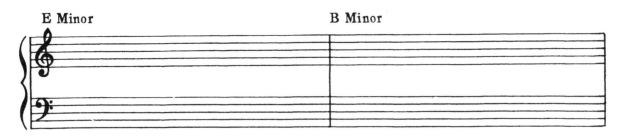

WORK SHEET

On the staves below, write the given RELATIVE MINOR SCALES (HARMONIC form), with key signature, one octave, ascending.   Mark half-steps.   Play until familiar.

E Minor   B Minor

F# Minor   C# Minor

G# Minor   Eb Minor

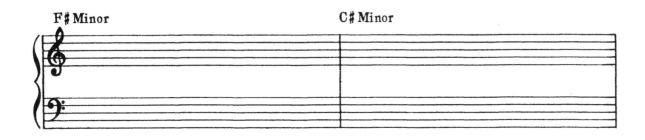
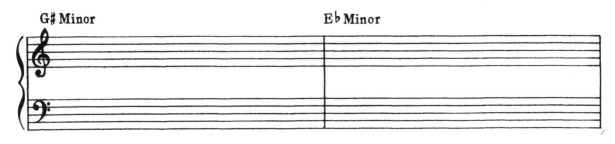

9

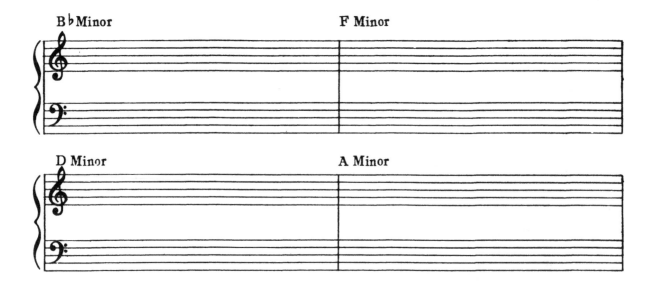

Find in piano literature examples of the HARMONIC MINOR SCALE.

LESSON 10
Melodic Minor

The MELODIC MINOR is an altered minor, with a raised 6th and 7th ascending, and a lowered 7th and 6th descending, using the relative major key signature.

Note: Half-steps between 2-3 and 7-8 ascending, 6-5 and 3-2 descending.

Write in 𝄞 and 𝄢: the D MINOR SCALE (MELODIC form) with key signature, one octave, ascending and descending. Mark the half-steps. Play until familiar.

Study Ex. 12 and 13.   Name and write key of each.   Circle MELODIC MINOR SCALES.   Play:

WORK SHEET

On the staves below, write the given RELATIVE MINOR SCALES (MELODIC form), with key signatures, one octave, ascending *and* descending. Mark half-steps. Play until familiar.

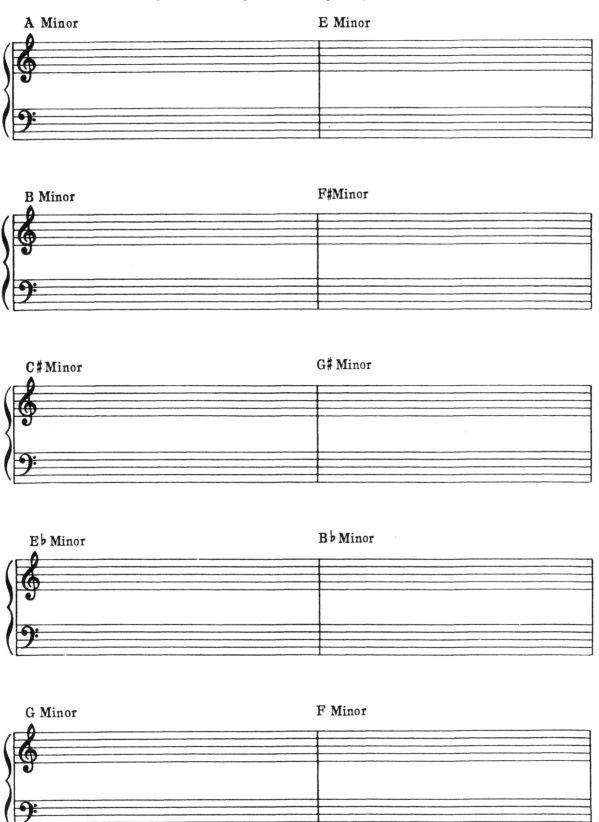

A Minor

E Minor

B Minor

F♯ Minor

C♯ Minor

G♯ Minor

E♭ Minor

B♭ Minor

G Minor

F Minor

Find in piano literature examples of the MELODIC MINOR SCALE.

11

LESSON 11
The Chromatic Scale

The CHROMATIC SCALE consists of all the black and white keys, played consecutively. It is composed of twelve half-steps, and can be used with any key signature.

Play the CHROMATIC SCALE from any pitch on the piano, until familiar.

Study Ex. 14 and 15.   Name and write key.   Circle CHROMATIC SCALE.   Play:

Key: ☐

VIVACE from SONATINA OP. 55, #1
F. Kuhlau

Key: ☐

CHROMATICS
Wallingford Riegger

N3167

LESSON 12
The Pentatonic Scale

The PENTATONIC SCALE is a five-tone scale (the five black keys on the piano, beginning with F♯). It may also be transposed.

Note: Whole tones except between 3-4 where there is a minor third.

Play a PENTATONIC SCALE from G, D, A, and B, until familiar.

Study Ex. 16 and 17. Name and write key. Circle PENTATONIC pattern. Play:

Key: ☐

THE YOUNG SWING PIANIST
Alexandre Tansman

Ex. 16

Key: ☐

TOUCHES NOIRES
Darius Milhaud

Ex. 17

LESSON 13
The Whole-Tone Scale

The WHOLE-TONE SCALE consists of six tones, a whole-step apart.

There are only 2 WHOLE-TONE SCALES on the keyboard.

Play the WHOLE-TONE SCALE from E or F until familiar.

Study Ex. 18 and 19. Circle WHOLE-TONE pattern. Play:

TRAFFIC DANCE
Robert Stoltze

Ex. 18

N3167

FIVE-FINGER EXERCISE
Bela Bartok

Ex. 19

Moderato

mf ¹*poco espr.*

Find in piano literature examples of CHROMATIC, PENTATONIC and WHOLE-TONE SCALES.

LESSON 14
The Medieval Modes

The MEDIEVAL MODES were the scales in use before our present MAJOR and MINOR scales. These latter may be dated from early in the seventeenth century. The MEDIEVAL MODES are also used extensively by contemporary composers.

MEDIEVAL MODES (Authentic)	RANGE	CHARACTERISTIC TONE
Dorian	D-D	B♮ (Raised 6th)
Phrygian	E-E	F♮ (lowered 2nd)
Lydian	F-F	B♮ (Raised 4th)
Mixo-lydian	G-G	F♮ (lowered 7th)
Aeolian (Natural minor)	A-A	G♮ (lowered 7th)
Ionian (Major)	C-C	none

The Dorian Mode

The range of the pure DORIAN MODE is from D to D on white keys. It may also be transposed.

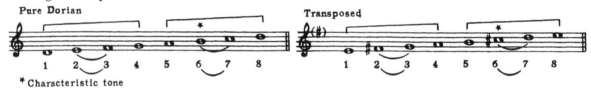

Pure Dorian   Transposed

*Characteristic tone

Study Ex. 20.   This composition uses the DORIAN MODE in its pure form.   Play:

MAZURKA RUSTIQUE, OP. 15, #1
A. Liadow

Allegro

Ex. 20

Study Ex. 21.   This composition uses the transposed DORIAN MODE.   The C♯ is the characteristic tone which distinguishes it from E MINOR.   Play:

No. 28
85 PIANO PIECES, Vol. 1
Bela Bartok

Parlando

simile

Ex. 21

LESSON 15
The Phrygian Mode

The range of the pure PHRYGIAN MODE is from E to E on white keys. It may also be transposed.

*Characteristic tone

Study Ex. 22. This composition uses the PHRYGIAN MODE in its pure form. Play:

No. 34
MIKROKOSMOS, Vol. 1
Bela Bartok

Copyright 1940 by Hawkes & Son Ltd., London. Used by permission of Boosey & Hawkes, New York, N.Y.

Study Ex. 23. This composition uses the transposed PHRYGIAN MODE. The D♮ is the characteristic tone which distinguishes it from C♯ MINOR. Play:

MAZURKA, OP. 41, #1
Frederic Chopin

LESSON 16
The Lydian Mode

The range of the pure LYDIAN MODE is from F to F on the white keys. It may also be transposed:

*Characteristic tone

Study Ex. 24 and 25. These compositions use the pure LYDIAN MODE. Play:

IT'S A BRIGHT MORNING
John Moore

Permission for reprint granted by Boston Music Co., New York, N.Y.

N3167

LESSON 17
The Mixolydian Mode

The range of the pure MIXOLYDIAN MODE is from G to G on white keys. It may also be transposed.

Study Ex. 26. The composer creates the MIXOLYDIAN SCALE by writing F♮ in a G MAJOR key.
Play:

In Ex. 27, E♮ is the characteristic tone.   Play:

N3167

LESSON 18
The Aeolian Mode (Natural Minor)

The range of the pure AEOLIAN MODE (NATURAL MINOR) is from A to A on white keys. It may also be transposed.

Study Ex. 28 and 29. These compositions use the pure form of the AEOLIAN MODE. Play:

LULLABY
Ernest Bloch

ETUDE
D. Kabalevsky

Find in contemporary piano literature, examples of MODAL writing.

N3167

PART II
Intervals

An INTERVAL is the distance between two tones. These tones may be sounded together (harmonically) or separately (melodically).

The INTERVALS in the Major Scale, reading up from the first scale step, are:

| PERFECT PRIME | MAJOR 2ND | MAJOR 3RD | PERFECT 4TH | PERFECT 5TH | MAJOR 6TH | MAJOR 7TH | PERFECT OCTAVE |

LESSON 19
The Major Second

The MAJOR SECOND (WHOLE STEP) is a large second (1-2 in the Major Scale). Note the spacing on the staff.

Space, up or down 1 line: Line, up or down 1 space:

Play, looking at the keyboard.

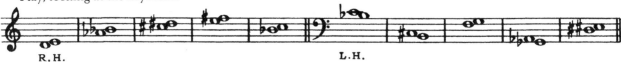

Play. Do not look at keyboard. Feel your way.

Circle 3 MAJOR SECONDS (MELODIC) in Ex. 30. Play:

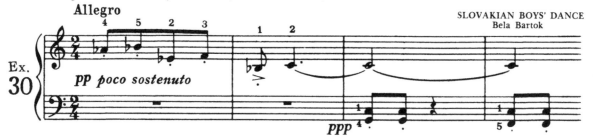

SLOVAKIAN BOYS' DANCE
Bela Bartok

From 10 EASY PIECES, BELA BARTOK. Edited by Denes Agay. Copyright 1950 by Leeds Music Corp. Reprinted by permission. All rights reserved.

Circle 4 MAJOR SECONDS (HARMONIC) in Ex. 31. Play:

FIESTA
J. Turina

18

Write MAJOR SECONDS up and down from given notes.

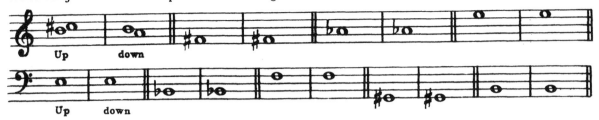

Find in piano literature examples of the MAJOR SECOND.

LESSON 20
The Minor Second

The MINOR SECOND (HALF-STEP or small second), is one half-step smaller than the MAJOR SECOND. The spacing on the staff is the same:

Play, looking at the keyboard.

Play. Do not look at keyboard. Feel your way.

Circle 4 MINOR SECONDS (MELODIC) in Ex. 32. Play:

Circle 3 MAJOR SECONDS and 6 MINOR SECONDS (HARMONIC) in Ex. 33. Play:

From MUSIC FOR CHILDREN, OP. 65, SERGE PROKOFIEFF. Edited with special annotations by Joseph Wolman. Copyright 1946, Leeds Music Corp. Reprinted by special permission. All rights reserved.

Write MAJOR and MINOR SECONDS *down* from the given notes.

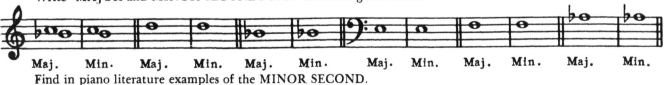

Maj.   Min.   Maj.   Min.   Maj.   Min.   Maj.   Min.   Maj.   Min.   Maj.   Min.

Find in piano literature examples of the MINOR SECOND.

19

N3167

LESSON 21
The Major Third

The MAJOR THIRD (large third) is 1-3 in the Major Scale. Note spacing on the staff.

Line, up or down 1 line: Space, up or down 1 space:

Play, looking at keyboard.

R.H.   L.H.

Play.   Do not look at keyboard.   Name the intervals as you play.

R.H.   L.H.

Circle 6 MAJOR THIRDS (3 HARMONIC, 3 MELODIC) in Ex. 34.   Play:

A TOYE
Giles Farnaby
(Ca. 1570-16-)

Ex. 34

Circle 2 MAJOR THIRDS and 2 MINOR THIRDS, (HARMONIC) in Ex. 35.   Play:

SONG OF THE VAGABOND
Bela Bartok

Ex. 35

Permission for reprint granted by G. Schirmer, Inc., New York, copyright owners.

Write MAJOR THIRDS up and down from given notes.

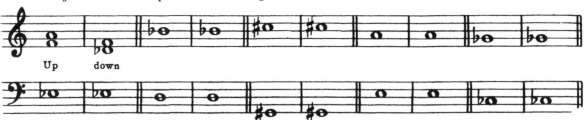

Up   down

Find in piano literature examples of the MAJOR THIRD.

LESSON 22
The Minor Third

The MINOR THIRD (small third) is one half-step smaller than the MAJOR THIRD. The spacing on the staff is the same.

Major third   Minor third   Minor third

N3167

Play, looking at keyboard.

Play.   Do not look at keyboard.   Name the intervals as you play.

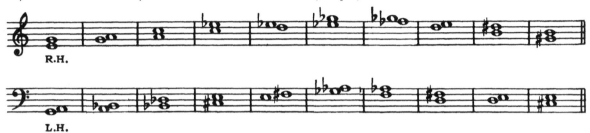

Circle at least 11 THIRDS (MAJOR and MINOR) in Ex. 36.   Play:

MENUETTO from LITTLE SUITE #1
Johann W. Hassler

Circle at least 12 THIRDS (MAJOR and MINOR) in Ex. 37.   Play:

GRIEVIN' ANNIE
Douglas Moore

Write MAJOR and MINOR THIRDS *down* from given notes.

Maj.   Min.   Maj.   Min.   Maj.   Min.   Maj.   Min.   Maj.   Min.   Maj.   Min.   Maj.   Min.

Find in piano literature examples of MAJOR and MINOR THIRDS.

N3167

LESSON 23
The Perfect Fourth

The PERFECT FOURTH is 1-4 in the Major Scale. Note spacing on the staff.

Line, up or down 2 spaces: Space, up or down 2 lines:

Play, looking at keyboard.

R.H.   L.H.

Play.   Do not look at keyboard.   As you play, name the intervals.

R.H.   L.H.

Circle 5 PERFECT FOURTHS (HARMONIC) in Ex. 38.   Play:

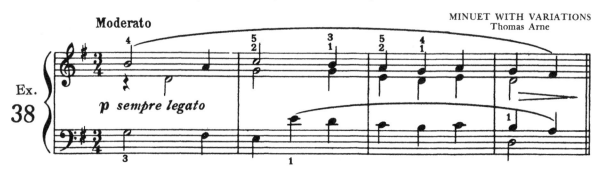

MINUET WITH VARIATIONS
Thomas Arne

Circle 12 PERFECT FOURTHS (HARMONIC) in Ex. 39.   Play:

DAWN from UNE JOURNEE
Darius Milhaud

Copyright 1947 by Mercury Music Corp., New York, N. Y. Reproduced by permission.

Circle 12 PERFECT FOURTHS (HARMONIC) and 5 PERFECT FOURTHS (MELODIC) in Ex. 40.
This composition is built on a ground bass (ostinato) (see page 71) of PERFECT FOURTHS.   Play:

WITH TRUMPETS
AND DRUMS
Isadore Freed

Copyright 1936 by Carl Fischer, Inc., New York, N. Y. Reprinted by permission.

22

N3167

Write PERFECT FOURTHS *up* and *down* from given notes.

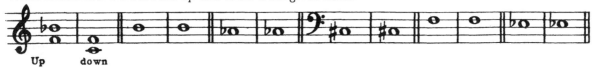

Up   down

Find in piano literature examples of the PERFECT FOURTH

LESSON 24
The Perfect Fifth

The PERFECT FIFTH is 1-5 in the Major Scale. Note spacing on the staff.

Line, up or down 2 lines: Space, up or down 2 spaces:

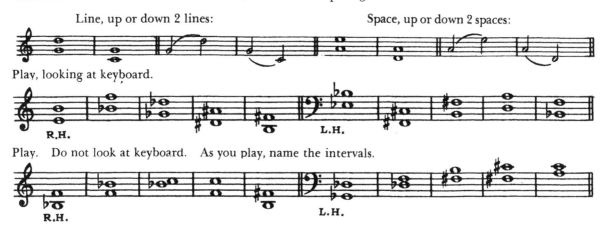

Play, looking at keyboard.

R.H.   L.H.

Play. Do not look at keyboard. As you play, name the intervals.

R.H.   L.H.

Circle 4 PERFECT FIFTHS (HARMONIC) in Ex. 41. Name all MELODIC intervals. Play·

STATEMENT from LITTLE PIANO BOOK
Vincent Persichetti

Ex. 41

f il ritmo sempre | *molto preciso*

Permission for reprint granted by Elkan-Vogel, Inc., Philadelphia, Pa. Copyright owners.

Circle 4 PERFECT FIFTHS (MELODIC). Name all other intervals in Ex. 42. Play:

#18 from SCHOOL OF VELOCITY, OP 141
C. Gurlitt

Ex. 42

Allegretto

Diminished fifth

Circle all PERFECT FIFTHS (HARMONIC) in Ex. 43. Play:

THE MECHANICAL DOLL
D. Shostakovitch

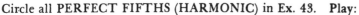

Write PERFECT FOURTHS and PERFECT FIFTHS *up* from given notes.

Find in piano literature examples of the PERFECT FIFTH.

LESSON 25
The Major Sixth

The MAJOR SIXTH is 1-6 in the Major Scale. Note spacing on the staff.

Line, up or down 3 spaces: Space, up or down 3 lines:

Play, looking at keyboard.

Play.   Do not look at keyboard.   As you play, name the intervals.

Circle 16 MAJOR SIXTHS (HARMONIC) in Ex. 44.   Play:

POLONAISE from ANNA
M. Bach, Notebook

24

Circle 6 MAJOR SIXTHS (MELODIC) in Ex. 45.   Play:

Write MAJOR SIXTHS *up* and *down* from given notes.

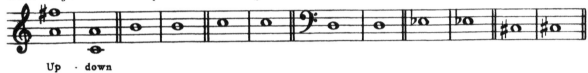

Up · down

Find in piano literature examples of the MAJOR SIXTH.

LESSON 26
The Minor Sixth

The MINOR SIXTH is one half-step smaller than the MAJOR SIXTH. The spacing on the staff is the same as in the MAJOR SIXTH.

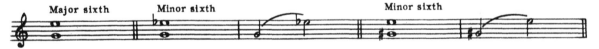

Play, looking at keyboard.

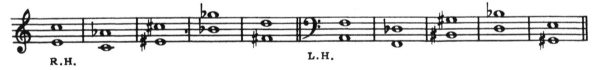

Play.   Do not look at keyboard.   As you play, name the intervals.

Circle at least 5 MAJOR and MINOR SIXTHS in Ex. 46.   Play:

25

Circle 4 MINOR SIXTHS (HARMONIC) in Ex. 47. Play:

Allegro moderato

MENUET IN C
Ludwig van Beethoven

Ex.
47

Write MAJOR and MINOR SIXTHS *down* from given notes:

Maj.   Min.   Maj.   Min.   Maj.   Min.   Maj.   Min.   Maj.   Min.   Maj.   Min.

Find in piano literature examples of MAJOR and MINOR SIXTHS.

LESSON 27
The Major Seventh

The MAJOR SEVENTH is 1-7 in the Major Scale. Note spacing on the staff.

Line, up or down 3 lines: Space, up or down 3 spaces:

Play, looking at keyboard.

R.H.   L.H.

Play.   Do not look at keyboard.   As you play, name the intervals.

R.H.   L.H.

Circle 1 MAJOR SEVENTH in Ex. 48.   Name all other intervals.   Play:

PRESTO from SONATA IN G (K# 283)
Wolfgang A. Mozart

Presto

Ex.
48

N3167

Circle 4 SIXTHS and 1 MAJOR SEVENTH (HARMONIC) in Ex. 49. Play:

SARABANDE, D MINOR FRENCH SUITE
Johann S. Bach

Write MAJOR SEVENTHS *up* and *down* from the given pitches:

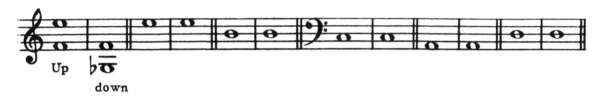

Find in piano literature examples of the MAJOR SEVENTH.

LESSON 28
The Minor Seventh

The MINOR SEVENTH is one half-step smaller than the MAJOR SEVENTH, or one whole-step smaller than the octave. Spacing on the staff is the same as that of the MAJOR SEVENTH.

Play, looking at keyboard.

Play. Do not look at keyboard. As you play, name the intervals.

Circle 4 MINOR SEVENTHS (MELODIC) in Ex. 50. Name all other intervals. Play:

STROLLING MUSICIANS, OP. 31
V. Rebikov

Permission for reprint granted by G. Schirmer, Inc., New York, copyright owners.

27

N3167

Circle 2 MAJOR SEVENTHS, 3 MINOR SEVENTHS in Ex. 51.   Play:

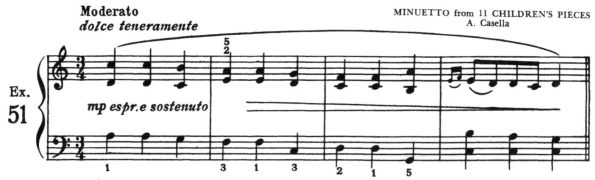

Moderato
dolce teneramente

MINUETTO from 11 CHILDREN'S PIECES
A. Casella

Ex. 51

mp espr. e sostenuto

Write MAJOR and MINOR SEVENTHS *down* from given notes:

Maj.   Min.   Maj.   Min.   Maj.   Min.   Maj.   Min.   Maj.   Min.   Maj.   Min.

Find in piano literature examples of MAJOR and MINOR SEVENTHS.

LESSON 29
The Unison and the Octave

The UNISON, or PERFECT PRIME, is a doubling or repetition of the same note (1-1 in the scale). The OCTAVE is 1-8 in the scale. Note spacing on the staff.

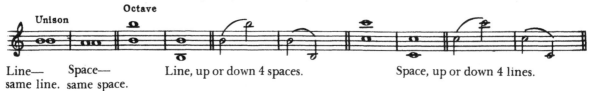

Unison   Octave

Line—   Space—   Line, up or down 4 spaces.   Space, up or down 4 lines.
same line. same space.

Play, looking at keyboard.

R.H.   L.H.

Play.   Do not look at keyboard.   As you play, name the intervals.

R.H.   L.H.

Circle all OCTAVES (MELODIC) in Ex. 52.   Play:

Musette

MUSETTE, LITTLE SUITE #3
Leopold Mozart

Ex. 52

f

p

N3167

Circle 4 UNISONS in Ex. 53.   Play:

LINE AND POINT
Bela Bartok

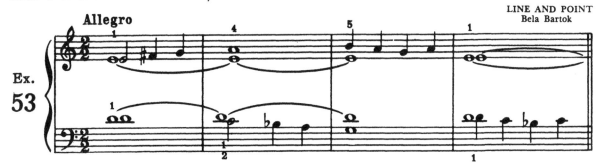

Circle 7 OCTAVES (HARMONIC) and 3 MAJOR SIXTHS (MELODIC) in Ex. 54.   Play:

ALLEGRETTO
G. M. Monn

Write PERFECT OCTAVES and UNISONS *down* from the given notes:

Find in piano literature examples of OCTAVES and UNISONS

LESSON 30
The Diminished Seventh

The DIMINISHED SEVENTH is one half-step smaller than a MINOR SEVENTH. On the piano it is the same in size and sound as the MAJOR SIXTH. The spacing on the staff is that of a seventh:

Play, looking at keyboard.

Play.   Do not look at keyboard.   As you play, name the intervals.

N3167

Circle 2 DIMINISHED SEVENTHS (MELODIC) in Ex. 55. Note how the SIXTHS in measures 2 and 4 are the same as the DIMINISHED SEVENTHS in sound and size on the keyboard. Play:

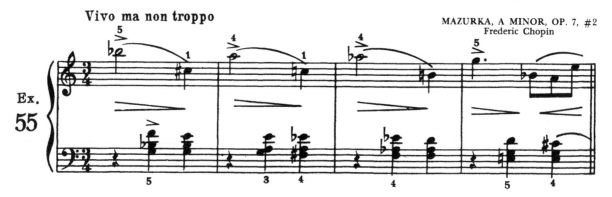

Circle 1 DIMINISHED SEVENTH and 1 MINOR SEVENTH in Ex. 56. Play:

Find in piano literature examples of the DIMINISHED SEVENTH.

LESSON 31
The Diminished Fifth

The DIMINISHED FIFTH is one half-step smaller than the PERFECT FIFTH (7 up to 4 in the Major Scale). Spacing on the staff is that of a fifth.

Play, looking at keyboard.

Play the following drill of the DIMINISHED FIFTH and its resolution to a THIRD (MAJOR or MINOR).

N3167

Circle all DIMINISHED FIFTHS in Ex. 57. Play:

NURSE'S TALE, OP. 109 #9
A. Gretchaninoff

Circle 4 DIMINISHED FIFTHS (HARMONIC) in Ex. 58. Play:

From SONATA IN D MINOR
Johann Adolph Hasse

Find in piano literature examples of the DIMINISHED FIFTH.

LESSON 32
The Augmented Fourth

The AUGMENTED FOURTH is one-half step larger than the PERFECT FOURTH (4 up to 7 in the Major Scale). On the piano keyboard it is the same size as the DIMINISHED FIFTH. Spacing on the staff is that of a fourth.

Play, looking at keyboard.

Play the following drill of the AUGMENTED FOURTH and its resolution to a SIXTH, (MAJOR or MINOR).

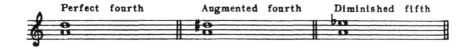

N3167

Circle 1 DIMINISHED FIFTH and 1 AUGMENTED FOURTH in Ex. 59.   To what intervals do they resolve?   Play:

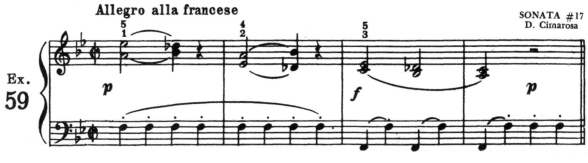

Name all intervals in Ex. 60.   Play:

Find in piano literature examples of the AUGMENTED FOURTH.

N3167

PART III
Triads and Seventh Chords

LESSON 33
Major Triads—Root Position

The MAJOR TRIAD is a three-tone chord built in thirds. It contains a MAJOR THIRD plus a MINOR THIRD, reading up from the root.

Play the following MAJOR TRIADS, root position, up and down the keyboard. (The Root is the lowest note of the TRIAD).

BROKEN, (Melodic):   BLOCKED, (Harmonic):

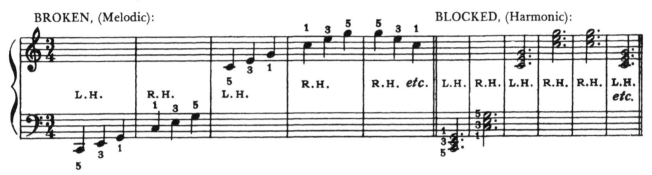

Play the above in all MAJOR KEYS. Check below when done.

		SHARPS									
C											
	1	2	3	4	5	6	7				
	G	D	A	E	B	F#	C#				
					Cb	Gb	Db	Ab	Eb	Bb	F
					7	6	5	4	3	2	1
						FLATS					

LESSON 34
Major Triads, Root Position, Played Chromatically

Play the following MAJOR TRIADS in root position, up and down the keyboard. Also play each TRIAD hand over hand, solid and broken as in Lesson 33.

Say: C Major Db Major *etc.*

N3167

LESSON 35
Minor Triads—Root Position

The MINOR TRIAD contains a MINOR THIRD plus a MAJOR THIRD, reading up from the root.

Play the following MINOR TRIADS in root position, up and down the keyboard.

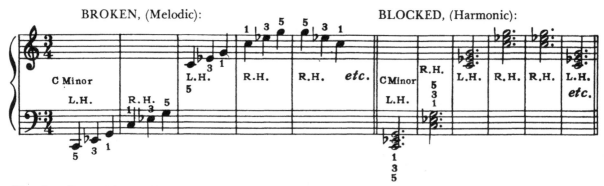

Play in all MINOR KEYS. Check below when done.

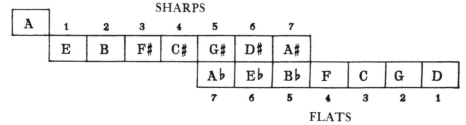

LESSON 36
Minor Triads, Root Position, Played Chromatically

Play the following MINOR TRIADS in root position, up and down the keyboard:

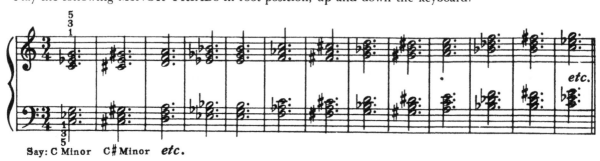

LESSON 37
Examples of Major and Minor Triads, Root Position

Play Ex. 61.   Play the TRIADS in blocked form. Name each (letter-name and Major or Minor quality).

34

N3167

Play Ex. 62. Name each TRIAD (letter-name and Major or Minor quality).

DANCE ON THE LAWN
D. Kabalevsky

Find in piano literature examples of MAJOR and MINOR TRIADS, Root Position.

LESSON 38
Major Triads—All Positions

Play the following MAJOR TRIADS in all positions, up and down the keyboard.

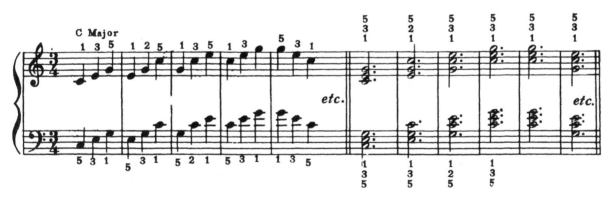

Play in all MAJOR KEYS. Check below when done.

				SHARPS						
1	2	3	4	5	6	7				
G	D	A	E	B	F#	C#				
				Cb	Gb	Db	Ab	Eb	Bb	F
				7	6	5	4	3	2	1

FLATS

N3167

Play Ex. 63. Block Left Hand.   Name all TRIADS (letter-name and Major or Minor quality).

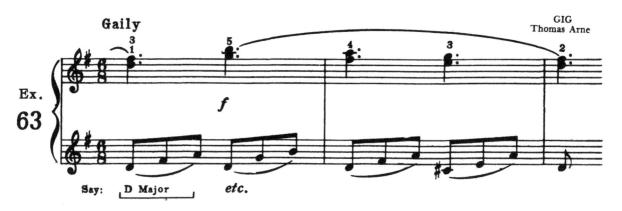

Play Ex. 64. Block the TRIADS.   Name each (letter-name and Major or Minor quality).

LESSON 39
Minor Triads—All Positions

Play the following MINOR TRIADS in all positions, up and down the keyboard.

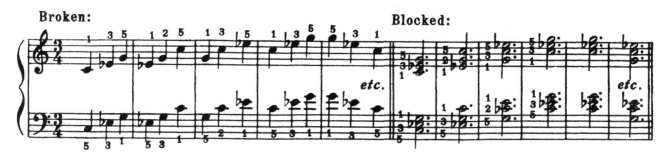

Play in all MINOR KEYS.   Check below when done.

		SHARPS										
A		1	2	3	4	5	6	7				
	E	B	F♯	C♯	G♯	D♯	A♯					
					A♭	E♭	B♭	F	C	G	D	
					7	6	5	4	3	2	1	
						FLATS						

N3167

Play Ex. 65. Name all TRIADS in 𝄞 and 𝄢: (letter-name and Major or Minor quality).

COQUETRY, OP. 47, #3
Stephen Heller

Find in piano literature examples of MAJOR and MINOR TRIADS, ALL POSITIONS.

LESSON 40
Triads—All Qualities

The AUGMENTED TRIAD contains 2 Major Thirds. The DIMINISHED TRIAD contains 2 Minor Thirds.

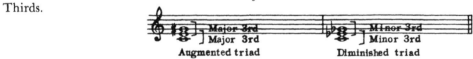

Play in all keys, ascending chromatically:

Say: Major,   Augmented, Major, Minor, Diminished,   Major,   Augmented, Major, Minor, Diminished, *etc.*

Play Ex. 66. Find 1 MAJOR TRIAD, 1 DIMINISHED TRIAD.

MINUETTO
D. Scarlatti

N3167

Play Ex. 67. By combining Left hand with Right hand, find 1 AUGMENTED TRIAD, 2 DIMINISHED TRIADS, 1 MAJOR TRIAD, 1 MINOR TRIAD.

Play Ex. 68. Name all CHORDS

Say: **G Major G Augmented** *etc.*

Find in piano literature examples of TRIADS, ALL QUALITIES.

LESSON 41
Major Triads—Root on Top

Play the following MAJOR TRIADS (Root on top) up and down the keyboard.

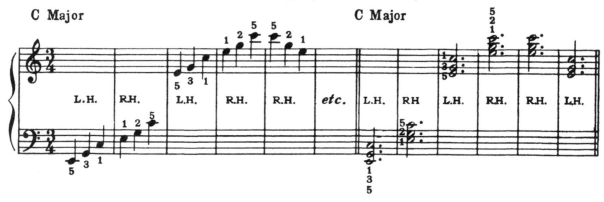

Using the first-measure patterns given below, play the above drills in all MAJOR KEYS.

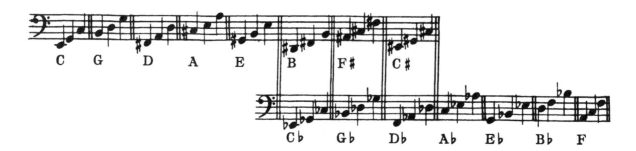

LESSON 42
Major Triads, Root on Top, Played Chromatically

Play the following MAJOR TRIADS (Root on top) up and down the keyboard. As you play, name all CHORDS (letter-name and quality).

Say: C Major Db Major *etc.*

Play Ex. 69. Block. Name all CHORDS (letter-name and quality).

VIVACE from SONATA IN D
P. Paradisi

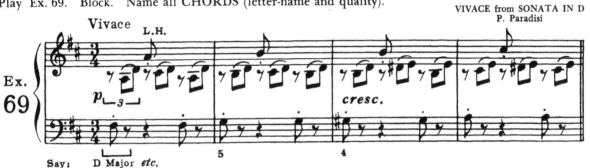

Say: D Major *etc.*

LESSON 43
Minor Triads—Root on Top

Play the following MINOR TRIADS (Root on top) up and down the keyboard.

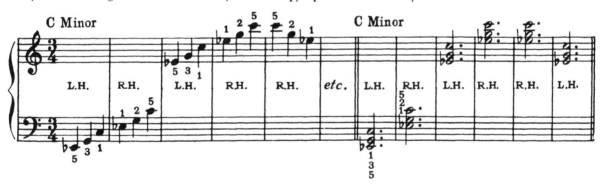

Using the first-measure patterns given below play the above drills in all MINOR KEYS.

39

LESSON 44
Minor Triads, Root on Top, Played Chromatically

Play the following MINOR TRIADS (Root on top) up and down the keyboard. As you play, name all CHORDS (letter-name and quality).

Say: C Minor C♯ Minor *etc.*

Play Ex. 70. Block the CHORDS. Name each (letter-name and quality). There are 2 DIMINISHED TRIADS in this example.

GIGUE from SONATA IN D
B. Galuppi

Say: D Major A Major *etc.*

Play Ex. 71. Name all TRIADS (letter-name and quality).

TOCCATINA
D. Kabalevsky

Play Ex. 72 and 73. Name each CHORD (letter-name and quality).

SARABANDE
Leopold Mozart

N3167

Find in piano literature examples of MAJOR, MINOR, AUGMENTED, DIMINISHED TRIADS with Root on top.

LESSON 45
Major Triads—Root in the Middle

Play the following MAJOR TRIADS (Root in the middle) up and down the keyboard.

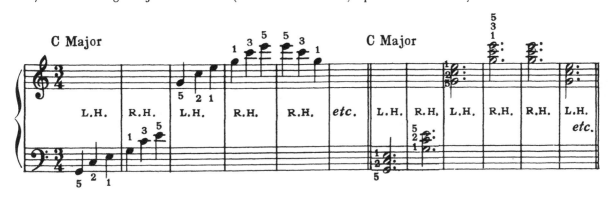

Play the above drills in all MAJOR KEYS.

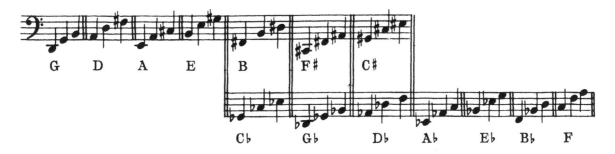

41

LESSON 46
Major Triads, Root in the Middle, Played Chromatically

Play the following MAJOR TRIADS (Root in the middle) up and down the keyboard. As you play, name all CHORDS (letter-name and quality).

Say: C Major   Db Major *etc.*

Play Ex. 74. Block the CHORDS.   Name each (letter-name and quality).

FANTASIA
Leopold Mozart

Moderato con espressione

Ex. 74

LESSON 47
Minor Triads—Root in the Middle

Play the following MINOR TRIADS (Root in the middle) up and down the keyboard:

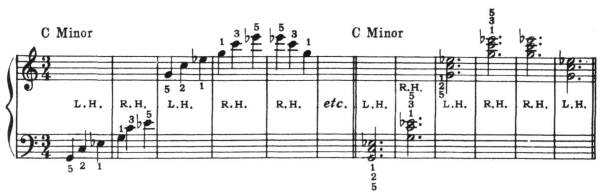

Using the first-measure patterns given below play the above drills in all MINOR KEYS.

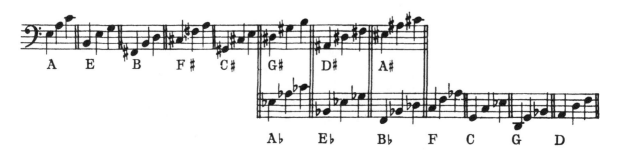

A   E   B   F#   C#   G#   D#   A#

Ab   Eb   Bb   F   C   G   D

N3167

LESSON 48
Minor Triads, Root in the Middle, Played Chromatically

Play the following MINOR TRIADS (Root in the middle) up and down the keyboard.
As you play, name all CHORDS (letter-name and quality):

Say: C Minor C♯ Minor *etc.*

Play Ex. 75. Block the left hand. Name each CHORD (letter-name and quality).

A SHORT STORY
D. Kabalevsky

Andantino cantabile

Ex.
75

mf

Find in piano literature examples of MINOR, AUGMENTED, DIMINISHED TRIADS with root as the middle note.

LESSON 49
Mixed Drill—Major

Harmonize the DESCENDING CHROMATIC SCALE with the nearest MAJOR TRIAD at hand.

Say: C   B   B♭   A   A♭   G   F♯   F   E   E♭   D   D♭   C
Major

D♭   D   E♭   E   F   F♯   G   A♭   A   B♭   B   C

N3167

LESSON 50
Mixed Drill—Minor

Say: C Minor etc.

LESSON 51
The Dominant Seventh—Played Chromatically

The DOMINANT SEVENTH CHORD consists of a MAJOR TRIAD and the interval of a MINOR SEVENTH.

Play the following DOMINANT SEVENTHS ROOT POSITION up and down the keyboard. As you play, name each CHORD.

Say: C7   C#7   D7   etc.

LESSON 52
Dominant Sevenths—All Positions

Play the following drill of the DOMINANT SEVENTH and its POSITIONS up and down the keyboard.

Play from every scale-step, C#, D, Eb etc.

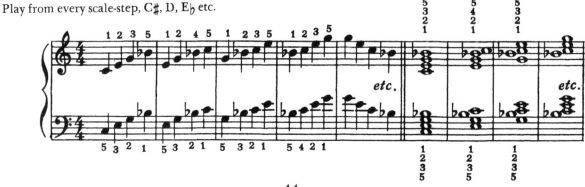

N3167

Play Ex. 76.   Name (letter-name) all DOMINANT SEVENTHS.

ECOSSAISE IN G
Franz Schubert

Say: B 7   etc.

Play Ex. 77.   By combining both hands, find 2 DOMINANT SEVENTHS.   Notice how each resolves to a TRIAD.

SCHERZANDO
Ludwig van Beethoven

Play Ex. 78 and 79. Name all chords. Notice how each DOMINANT SEVENTH resolves to a TRIAD.

GIGUE IN G MINOR
Jean B. Loeillet

WALTZ IN A FLAT
Franz Schubert

Find in piano literature examples of DOMINANT SEVENTHS, ALL POSITIONS.

N3167

LESSON 53
The Diminished Seventh—Played Chromatically

The DIMINISHED SEVENTH CHORD consists of a DIMINISHED TRIAD and the interval of a DIMINISHED SEVENTH:

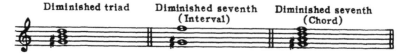

Play the following DIMINISHED SEVENTHS up and down the keyboard. There are only *three* DIMINISHED SEVENTHS (see ⌐⌐). All others are the same chords in various positions.

LESSON 54
Diminished Sevenths—All Positions

Play the following DIMINISHED SEVENTHS in ALL POSITIONS up and down the keyboard.

Play from C♯, D and D♯:

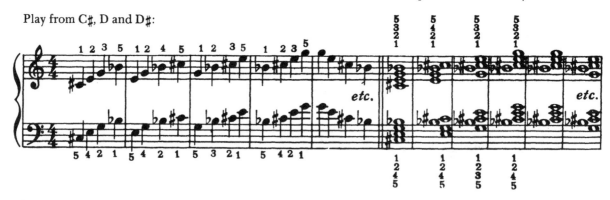

Play Ex. 80.   Name all DIMINISHED SEVENTHS.   Notice how each resolves to a TRIAD

PRAELUDIUM #1 from
THE WELL-TEMPERED CLAVICHORD
J. S. Bach

Find in piano literature examples of DIMINISHED SEVENTHS in ALL POSITIONS.

46

LESSON 55
Other Types of Seventh Chords

The MAJOR SEVENTH CHORD consists of a MAJOR TRIAD and the interval of a MAJOR SEVENTH. The MINOR SEVENTH CHORD consists of a MINOR TRIAD and the interval of a MINOR SEVENTH. The HALF-DIMINISHED SEVENTH CHORD consists of a DIMINISHED TRIAD and the interval of a MINOR SEVENTH.

Play in all keys.

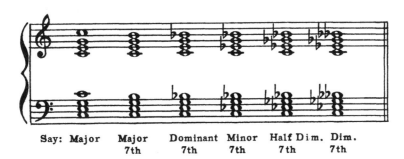

Say: Major   Major   Dominant   Minor   Half Dim.   Dim.
            7th   7th   7th   7th   7th

Play Ex. 81. Name: a DIMINISHED SEVENTH, a MAJOR SEVENTH, a HALF-DIMINISHED SEVENTH, a DOMINANT SEVENTH.

LITTLE PRELUDE IN C MINOR
Johann S. Bach

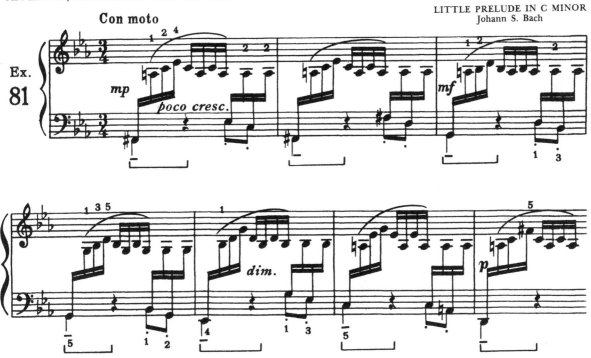

Find in piano literature examples of MAJOR SEVENTH CHORD, MINOR SEVENTH CHORD, HALF-DIMINISHED SEVENTH CHORD.

N3167

PART IV
Cadences and Harmonizations

THE CADENCE

The **CADENCE** is a chord-progression written to punctuate the harmonic motion of a composition—to give a point of rest—temporary, or final. The **CADENCES** in PART IV are presented as keyboard drill. For a complete list of all types of **CADENCES**, see PART V, Lesson 80, Page 68.

LESSON 56
I IV V I In Major
(PREPARATORY DRILL)

Play and learn the names of the given Triads in the Major Scale. Notice the quality (MAJOR, MINOR, DIMINISHED) of each.

Play the following in all Major Keys.   Name the chords as you play, (letter-name and quality).

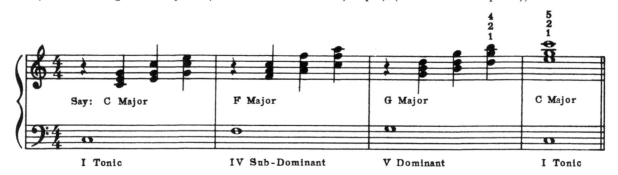

LESSON 57
I IV V I In Minor
(PREPARATORY DRILL)

Play and learn the names of the given Triads in the Harmonic Minor Scale. Notice the quality (MAJOR, MINOR, DIMINISHED, AUGMENTED) of each.

Play the following in all Minor Keys.   Name the chords as you play (letter-name and quality.) Notice that in a Minor Key I and IV are Minor, V remains Major.

48

N8167

Play the following in all Major Keys. Keep the COMMON TONE where marked (—). Notice how the other chord-tones move *down* in the scale and then *up*. Name each chord (letter-name and quality) as you play.

Play Ex. 82 and 83. Name each chord (letter-name and quality).

RONDOLETTO
Wolfgang A. Mozart

SOLDIERS MARCH
Robert Schumann

Find in piano literature examples of V and I in a MAJOR KEY.

Play the following in all Minor Keys. Notice that V in a Minor Key is Major. Name each chord (letter-name and quality).

49

N3167

Play Ex. 84 and 85.   Name each chord (letter-name and quality).

With a lilt, but not too quickly

A GIGGE
William Byrd

Ex. 84

Say: A Minor   etc.

A Minor: I   V   I

SOLFEGGIETTO
Karl Philip Emanuel Bach

Non troppo vivo

Ex. 85

C Minor: I   V   I   V

Find in piano literature examples of V and I in a MINOR KEY.

LESSON 60
I IV I In Major

Play the following in all Major Keys.   Keep the common tone (—).   Move the other tones *up* then *down*.
Name each chord as you play, (letter-name and quality).

Say: C Major F Major   C Major   etc.

I   IV   I   I   IV   I   I   IV   I   I   IV   I

Play Ex. 86 and 87.   Name each chord (letter-name and quality).

AT THE SPINNING WHEEL
Stephen Heller

Allegretto

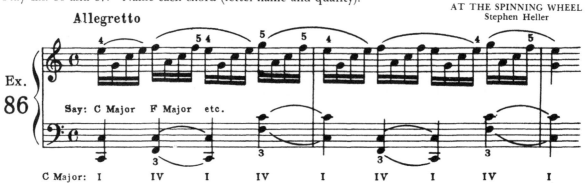

Ex. 86

Say: C Major   F Major   etc.

C Major: I   IV   I   IV   I   IV   I   IV   I

N3167

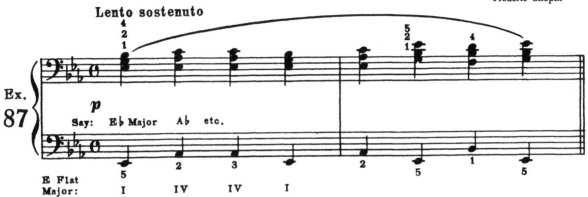

Find in piano literature examples of IV and I in a MAJOR KEY.

LESSON 61
I IV I In Minor

Play the following in all Minor Keys.   Name each chord (letter-name and quality).

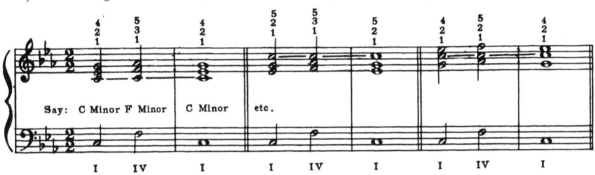

Play Ex. 88 and 89.   Name each chord (letter-name and quality).

AIR, from TOCCATA
Alessandro Scarlatti

THE SICK DOLL
P. Tschaikowsky

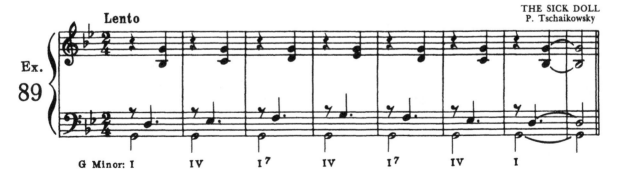

Find in piano literature examples of IV and I in a MINOR KEY.

51

I IV V I *In Major*

Play the following in all Major Keys. Keep the common tone where marked (—). Notice that, in moving from IV to V, the bass comes *up* and the other parts go *down*. Name each chord (letter-name and quality).

Play Ex. 90 and 91. Name each chord (letter-name and quality).

POLONAISE
Leopold Mozart

MENUETTO from VIENNESE SONATINA #6
Wolfgang A. Mozart

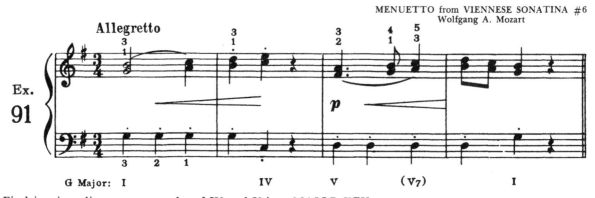

Find in piano literature examples of IV and V in a MAJOR KEY.

LESSON 63

I IV V I *In Minor*

Play the following in all Minor Keys. Name each chord (letter-name and quality).

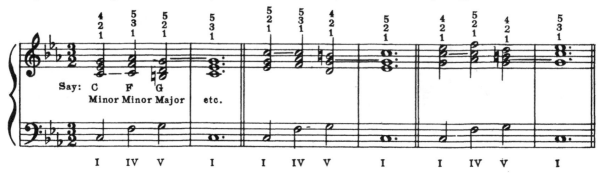

N3167

Play Ex. 92 and 93. Name each chord (letter-name and quality).

*In Baroque music, a composition written in minor may end on a Major Triad. The altered third of the chord is called the PICARDIAN THIRD.

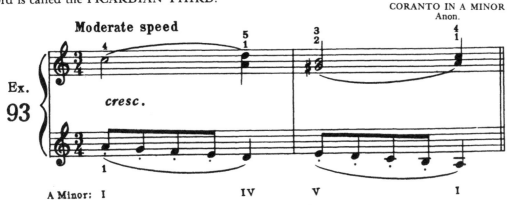

Find in piano literature examples of IV and V in a MINOR KEY.

LESSON 64
V7 In Major

Play the following in all Major Keys. Keep the common tone where marked (—). From IV to V7, notice the contrary motion between the bass and other parts. Name each chord (letter-name and quality) as you play.

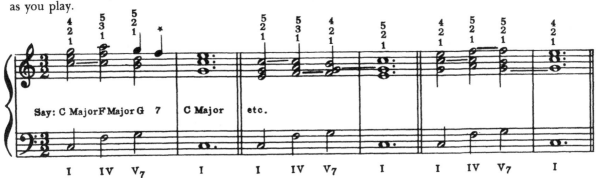

*The 7th originated as a passing-note, found a seventh above the Bass.
 Another name for V7 is DOMINANT SEVENTH.

Play Ex. 94 and 95. Name each chord (letter-name and quality) as you play.

53

Find in piano literature examples of V7 in a MAJOR KEY.

LESSON 65
V7 *In Minor*

Play the following in all Minor Keys.   Notice that I and IV become Minor, while V7 remains Dominant 7th.   Name each chord (letter-name and quality) as you play.

Play Ex. 96 and 97.   Name each chord (letter-name and quality) as you play.

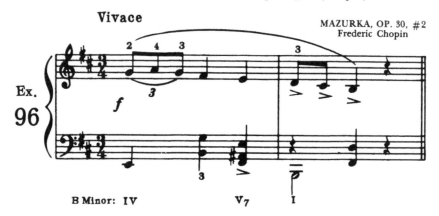

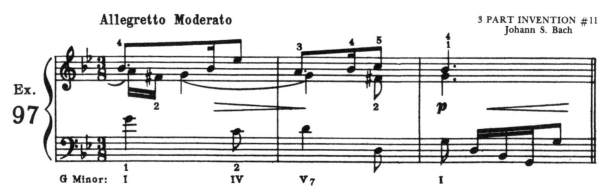

Find in piano literature examples of V7 in a MINOR KEY.

LESSON 66
The Meaning of Figured Bass Symbols

The Figures indicate the spelling of the Chord, reading up by intervals from the given Bass.

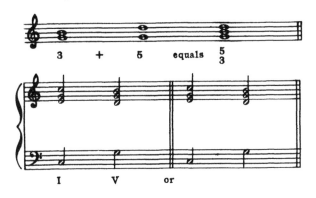

Any triad with root in the bass. The figures are often omitted. Thus, if no figures (Arabic) occur under the bass, it is assumed that the root is in the bass.

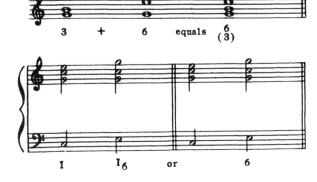

Any triad with third in the bass (First inversion). The 3 is often omitted. Thus, the Arabic number 6 under the bass means the First Inversion of a Triad.

Any triad with the fifth in the bass (Second inversion).

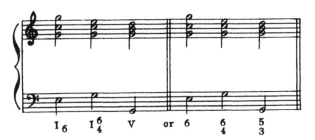

Any seventh chord (Root in the bass). The 3 is often omitted. A doubled third or root is indicated by 7 or 8.

$$\begin{matrix} & 5 \\ 3 & 7 \\ 3 & 3 \end{matrix}$$

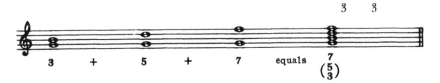

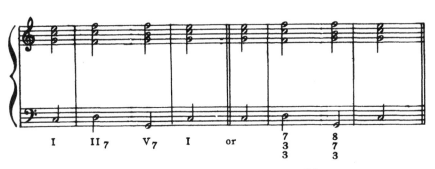

55

N3167

Any Seventh chord, First Inversion. The 3 is often omitted.

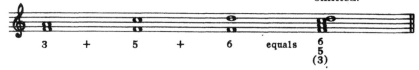

$$3 + 5 + 6 \text{ equals } \begin{smallmatrix}6\\5\\(3)\end{smallmatrix}$$

*87 indicates a passing-note effect—8ve of the chord moving to the 7th.

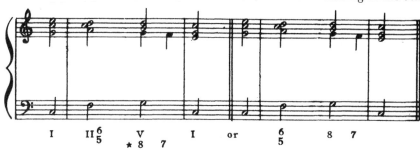

I II$\begin{smallmatrix}6\\5\end{smallmatrix}$ V I or $\begin{smallmatrix}6\\5\end{smallmatrix}$ 8 7
  *8 7

LESSON 67
II$_6$ In Major

The II$_6$ is the First Inversion of the II Chord. It is a Minor triad, in a Major Key. Play the following in all Major Keys. Name each chord (letter-name and quality) as you play.

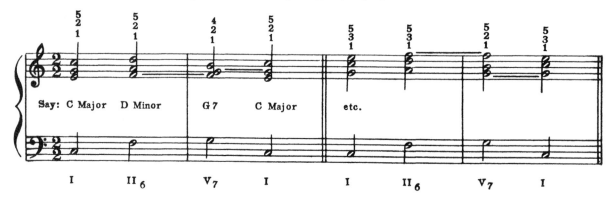

Say: C Major D Minor G 7 C Major etc.

I II$_6$ V$_7$ I I II$_6$ V$_7$ I

Play Ex. 98. As you play, analyze all chords (letter-name and quality).

SCHERZO, from SONATA OP. 28
Ludwig van Beethoven

Allegro vivace

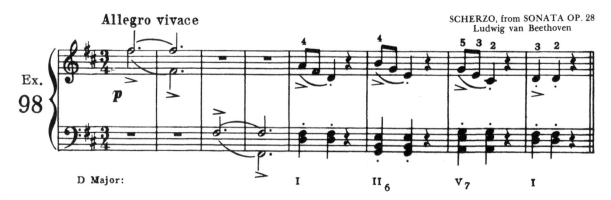

Ex. 98

D Major: I II$_6$ V$_7$ I

Find in piano literature an example of the use of II$_6$ in a MAJOR KEY.

56

N3167

LESSON 68
II₆ In Minor

The II$_6$ in Minor is Diminished.   Play the following in all Minor Keys.   Name each chord (letter-name and quality) as you play.

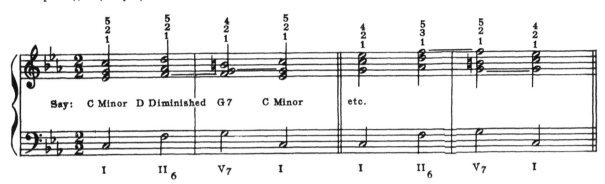

Say: C Minor   D Diminished   G 7   C Minor   etc.

I   II$_6$ V$_7$ I   I   II$_6$ V$_7$ I

Play Ex. 99.   As you play, name all chords (letter-name and quality).

TRIUMPH (Alla Marcia)
Stephen Heller

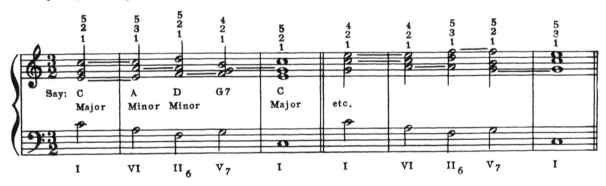

C Minor: I   II$_6$ V$_7$ I

Find in piano literature examples of II$_6$ in a MINOR KEY.

LESSON 69
VI In Major

Play the following in all Major Keys.   The VI is Minor in a Major Key.   Name each chord (letter-name and quality) as you play.

Say: C Major   A Minor   D Minor   G7   C Major   etc.

I   VI   II$_6$ V$_7$ I   I   VI   II$_6$ V$_7$ I

Play Ex. 100 and 101.   As you play, name all chords (letter-name and quality).

ALLEMANDE IN A
Ludwig van Beethoven

A Major: I   VI   II$_6$ V$_7$ I

57

A Major: V₇ I VI II₆ V I

Find in piano literature examples of VI in a MAJOR KEY.

LESSON 70
VI—Minor

Play the following in all Minor Keys.   The VI is Major in a Minor Key.   Name each chord (letter-name and quality) as you play.

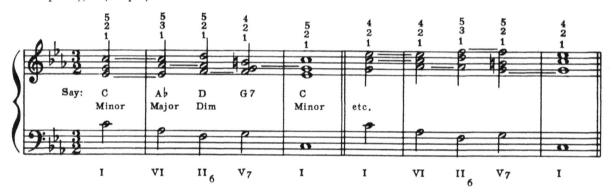

Say: C   Ab   D   G7   C
     Minor   Major   Dim   Minor   etc.

I   VI   II₆   V₇   I   I   VI   II₆   V₇   I

Play Ex. 102 and 103.   As you play, name all chords (letter-name and quality).

Find in piano literature examples of VI in a MINOR KEY.

58

N3167

LESSON 71
I$_4^6$ In Major

The I$_4^6$ is the Second Inversion of the Tonic Triad (5th in the bass). It often occurs before the V or V7 for a smoother progression at the cadence. Play the following in all Major Keys. Name each chord (letter-name and quality) as you play.

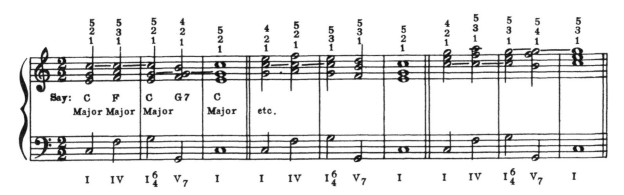

Say: C F C G7 C
Major Major Major Major etc.

I IV I$_4^6$ V$_7$ I   I IV I$_4^6$ V$_7$ I   I IV I$_4^6$ V$_7$ I

Play Ex. 104 and 105. As you play, name all chords (letter-name and quality).

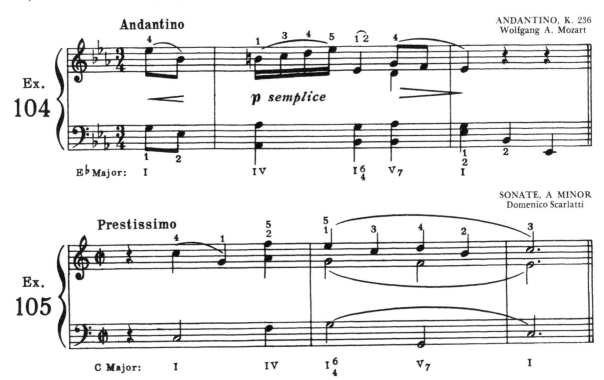

Ex. 104   **Andantino**

ANDANTINO, K. 236
Wolfgang A. Mozart

p semplice

E♭ Major: I   IV   I$_4^6$ V$_7$ I

Ex. 105   **Prestissimo**

SONATE, A MINOR
Domenico Scarlatti

C Major: I   IV   I$_4^6$ V$_7$ I

Find in piano literature examples of I$_4^6$ in a MAJOR KEY.

59

Play in all Minor Keys. Name each chord (letter-name and quality) as you play.

Say: C   F   C   G₇   C
     Minor Minor Minor   Minor   etc.

I   IV I_4^6 V₇   I   I   IV I_4^6 V₇   I   I   IV I_4^6 V₇   I

Play Ex. 106 and 107. As you play, name all chords (letter-name and quality).

Tempo di Mazurka

MAZURKA, OP. 39, #10
P. Tschaikowsky

Ex. 106

D Minor: IV I_4^6 V₇   I

Scherzando

ALLEGRETTO from MINUET IN F
Franz Schubert

Ex. 107

D Minor: V₇   I   V₇ of IV I_4^6 V₇   I

Find in piano literature examples of I_4^6 in a MINOR KEY.

LESSON 73
I_6 In Major and Minor

The I6 is the First Inversion of I (3rd in the bass), and is used for smoothness and variety. In this example the fifth is doubled. Play in all Major and Minor Keys. Name each chord (letter-name and quality) as you play.

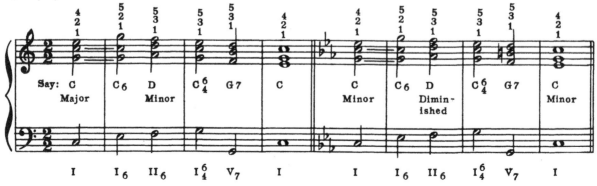

Say: C   C₆   D   C$_4^6$ G7   C   C   C₆   D   C$_4^6$ G7   C
     Major   Minor   Major   Minor   Dimin-   Minor
                                                       ished

I   I₆   II₆ I_4^6 V₇   I   I   I₆   II₆ I_4^6 V₇   I

N3167

Play Ex. 108 and 109.   As you play, name all chords (letter-name and quality).

MINUET TO DANCE
Johann Christoph Friedrich Bach

SONG WITHOUT WORDS #14
F. Mendelssohn

Allegro non troppo

Find in piano literature examples of I_6 in a MAJOR or MINOR KEY.

LESSON 74
III In Major

In a Major Key the III chord is Minor. Play in all Major Keys. Name each chord (letter-name and quality) as you play.

Play Ex. 110.   As you play, name all chords (letter-name and quality).

IMPROMPTU, OP. 90, #4
Franz Schubert

Allegro cantando

Find in piano literature examples of III in a MAJOR KEY.

61

LESSON 75
II$_5^6$ In Major and Minor

The II$_5^6$ is the First Inversion of the II$_7$ (3rd in the bass). In a Major Key it is a Minor Seventh; in a Minor Key it is a Half-diminished Seventh. Play in all Major and Minor Keys. Name each chord (letter-name and quality) as you play.

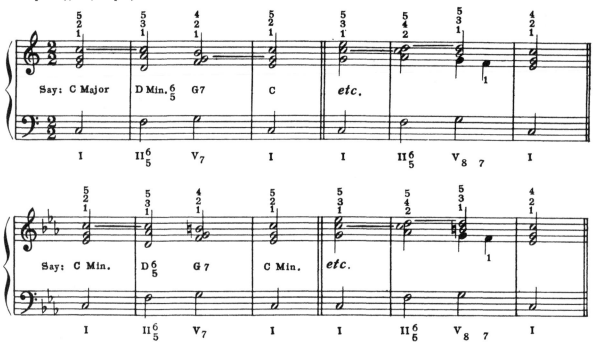

Play Ex. 111 and 112. Name all chords (letter-name and quality) as you play.

Find in piano literature examples of II$_5^6$ in a MAJOR or MINOR KEY.

62

LESSON 76
Major Scale Harmonization

The Major Scale may be harmonized in many different ways. In this version the VII6 is the First Inversion of VII (Diminished Triad).   Play in all Major Keys.   Name each chord (letter-name and quality).

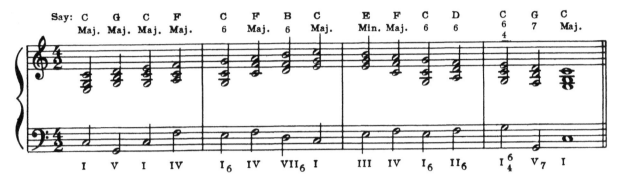

N3167

PART V
Form

LESSON 77
Introduction

The composer sometimes writes a passage preceding the first theme. Such material, when used at the beginning of the composition, is called INTRODUCTION.   Play Ex. 113.

The accompaniment figure used throughout the composition may be used as INTRODUCTION.

The composer may use the Ground Bass (Ostinato) (see p. 71) as the material for INTRODUCTION.

Find in piano literature examples of INTRODUCTION.

LESSON 78
Motive, Theme, Subject

A musical composition is built on one or more basic tonal ideas (MOTIVE, THEME or SUBJECT) which are stated, then developed. In analyzing much music where the statement is a short pattern, the term MOTIVE may be used. Play Ex. 116.

A HAPPY FAIRY TALE
Dimitri Shostakovitch

Ex. 116

From SIX CHILDREN'S PIECES, D. SHOSTAKOVITCH. Edited by Joseph Wolman. Copyright 1946 by Leeds Music Corp. Used by permission. All rights reserved.

The term THEME may be used in analyzing many small forms, as well as the Sonatina, Rondo and Sonata-allegro forms. Play Ex. 117 and 118.

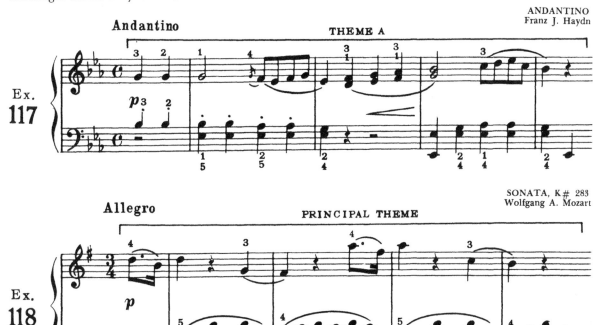

ANDANTINO
Franz J. Haydn

Ex. 117

SONATA, K# 283
Wolfgang A. Mozart

Ex. 118

(Note: Through usage, the terms PRINCIPAL THEME and SUBORDINATE THEME have come to mean, not only certain tonal ideas in Sonata-allegro form, but also the entire section built on those ideas.)

In the Fugue, the term SUBJECT is frequently used to indicate the basic idea on which the composition is built. Play Ex. 119.

LITTLE FUGUE #5
George Handel

Ex. 119

65

N3167

Music may develop *one* tonal idea (FUGUE, INVENTION). It may present *two* themes, which may be designated as A and B. These two musical ideas may be found in various arrangements: AABB; ABA; or AABBA. In large forms, *three* or more themes may be used in varying order: ABACDCA; ABACA etc. The possibilities are endless.

Find in piano literature examples of MOTIVE, THEME, SUBJECT.

LESSON 79
The Phrase

The PHRASE is the shortest complete and continuous musical thought, equivalent to a sentence or clause in speech. Phrases may vary from two to twenty or more measures in length. Play Ex. 120, 121, and 122.

A four-measure phrase:

Two-measure phrases:

From LITTLE SONG BOOK. Permission for reprint granted by Elkan-Vogel Co., Inc., Phila., Pa., copyright owners.

An eight-measure phrase:

N3167

Use the example below as a guide in analyzing the music you are studying. Mark each new Theme with a successive letter of the alphabet. Indicate phrases and phrase-lengths thus:

A,   4 measures
A¹, 4 measures
B,   2+2 measures
A¹, 4 measures

SONATINA, OP. 792
Carl Czerny

Find in piano literature examples of PHRASES of various lengths.

LESSON 80
Cadences—Points of Rest

A CADENCE is a chord progression written to punctuate the harmonic motion of a composition, to give a point of rest, temporary or final.

The PERFECT AUTHENTIC CADENCE is a complete and final close. The I chord has the 1st scale-step on top. Play Ex. 124.

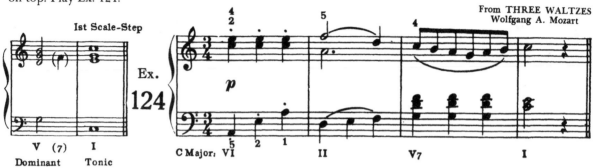

The IMPERFECT CADENCE is an incomplete close, still using V I, but ending with the 3rd or 5th scale-step on top. Play Ex. 125.

The SEMI-CADENCE is a half-cadence on V. Play Ex. 126.

The PLAGAL CADENCE is a IV I ("AMEN") progression. Play Ex. 127.

68

The EVADED or DECEPTIVE CADENCE substitutes VI, IV or other chords for I where a PERFECT AUTHENTIC CADENCE is expected. Play Ex. 128.

MINUET IN F
Wolfgang A. Mozart

Find in piano literature examples of:

1. PERFECT AUTHENTIC CADENCE
2. IMPERFECT CADENCE
3. SEMI-CADENCE
4. PLAGAL CADENCE
5. EVADED (DECEPTIVE) CADENCE

LESSON 81
Antecedent—Consequent

After a Phrase is stated, it is answered by another Phrase. The first Phrase is called the ANTECEDENT, the second, the CONSEQUENT. Play Ex. 129.

FIRST LOSS
Robert Schumann

When ANTECEDENT and CONSEQUENT begin alike, they are said to be in PARALLEL construction. Play Ex. 130.

MINUET IN C
Chr. F. Witte

When ANTECEDENT and CONSEQUENT begin differently, they are said to be in CONTRASTING construction. Play Ex. 131.

MINUET IN F
Joh. H. Buttstedt

Find in piano literature examples of:

1. ANTECEDENT PHRASE
2. CONSEQUENT PHRASE
3. Two PARALLEL PHRASES
4. Two CONTRASTING PHRASES

N3167

LESSON 82
Types of Accompaniment

The Theme or Motive may be accompanied by a pianistic figure or rhythmic pattern. Play Ex. 132, 133, and 134.

The THEME may be accompanied by a COUNTERPOINT, (another melody or melodies played simultaneously). Play Ex. 135.

COUNTERPOINT

The THEME may be presented with an ORGAN POINT (also called PEDAL POINT), (a note held or repeated while the harmony changes in other parts). Play Ex. 136.

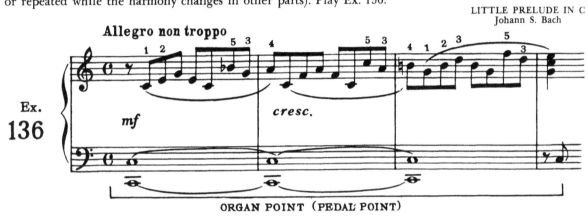

ORGAN POINT (PEDAL POINT)

The THEME may be accompanied by a GROUND BASS (OSTINATO)—a melodic pattern, or series of chords or intervals repeated many times in the bass. Play Ex. 137.

GROUND BASS (OSTINATO)

Find in piano literature examples of:
1. PIANISTIC FIGURE
2. COUNTERPOINT
3. ORGAN POINT, PEDAL POINT
4. GROUND BASS

N3167

LESSON 83
Repetition

A phrase is frequently stated, then repeated. If the REPETITION is exactly the same, it is called EXACT REPETITION. Play Ex. 138.

If the REPETITION is slightly changed, it is called MODIFIED REPETITION (see VARIATION). Play Ex. 139.

If the REPETITION is marked by a sudden change of dynamics from F to P, the composer is using the device of ECHO. Play Ex. 140.

N3167

The composer may also repeat a phrase in another octave, (CHANGE OF REGISTER).

Find in piano literature examples of:
1. EXACT REPETITION
2. MODIFIED REPETITION
3. ECHO
4. CHANGE OF REGISTER

LESSON 84
Imitation: Strict, Free, Canon

In contrapuntal music, a SUBJECT, MOTIVE or PHRASE may be imitated at the Octave, or at any other interval, by one or more voices. (STRICT IMITATION). Play Ex. 142.

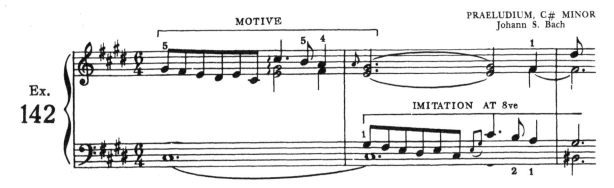

If the composer writes a Round for two or more voices, he is imitating the melody IN FULL (COMPLETE). This is called CANON. Play Ex. 143.

TWO-PART INVENTION #2
Johann S. Bach

Contrapuntal music contains many examples of FREE IMITATION, in which the interval structure of the MOTIVE or SUBJECT is altered. Play Ex. 144.

DUET IN A MINOR
Johann S. Bach

Find in contrapuntal piano literature examples of:
1. IMITATION AT THE OCTAVE (STRICT)
2. IMITATION IN FULL (CANON)
3. FREE IMITATION

N3167

LESSON 85
Imitation: Transposition, Inversion

A THEME, MOTIVE, or SUBJECT may be imitated in (transposed to) other keys. Play Ex. 145.

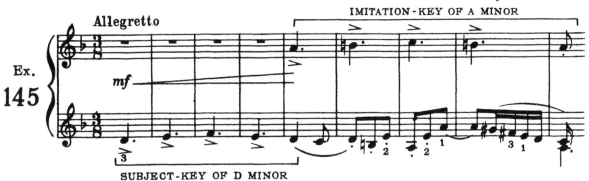

FUGHETTA D MINOR
Johann S. Bach

INVERSION: The melodic direction of a MOTIVE or SUBJECT may be reversed. Thus, descending melodic line becomes ascending and vice-versa. Play Ex. 146 and 147.

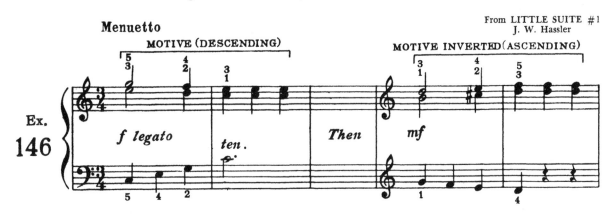

From LITTLE SUITE #1
J. W. Hassler

TWO-PART INVENTION #1
Johann S. Bach

Find in contrapuntal piano literature examples of:
   1. IMITATION IN (TRANSPOSITION TO) OTHER KEYS.
   2. INVERSION

N3167

LESSON 86
Variation

There are many ways in which the composer may vary the Theme. This common device keeps the listener's interest by adding something new, while reminding him of something old and familiar. Play Ex. 148.

SIMPLE MELODIC VARIATION, (see MODIFIED REPETITION).

Observe that, even in the course of a simple composition. VARIATION is needed.

The composer may write a set of VARIATIONS ON A THEME. Play Ex. 149.

Find in piano literature examples of VARIATION.

N3167

LESSON 87
Sequence, Fragments

When a motive is repeated on the *same* pitches, it is used in REPETITION. When it is repeated on *different* pitches, it is used in SEQUENCE says George A. Wedge.* Play Ex. 150.

A FRAGMENT is part of a MOTIVE, THEME or SUBJECT. FRAGMENTS are often used in SEQUENCE. Play Ex. 151.

Find in piano literature examples of:
1. SEQUENCE
2. FRAGMENTS

LESSON 88
Abbreviation, Expansion

If a section is repeated and shortened, the composer is using the device of ABBREVIATION. This is the A section of an A B A¹ form—16 measures. Play Ex. 152.

*"Keyboard Harmony," George A. Wedge, G. Schirmer, Inc., 1924.

77

N3167

Below is the A¹ section of the A B A¹ form. Notice how 16 measures are reduced to 8 measures.

In repetition, material may be lengthened or expanded. Play Ex. 153.

Allegro

#39, from
85 CHILDREN'S PIECES. VOL. 1
Bela Bartok

Ex.
153

Piú vivo

EXPANDED TO 8 MEASURES

Permission for reprint granted by G. Schirmer, Inc., New York, N. Y., copyright owners.

Find in piano literature examples of:
    1. ABBREVIATION
    2. EXPANSION

N3167

LESSON 89
Modulation—Change of Tonal Center

The process of going from one key or tonality to another is called MODULATION. Play Ex. 154.

KEY OF A MAJOR   TO KEY OF E MAJOR

In Contemporary music, because of the absence of Major and Minor keys, a CHANGE of TONAL CENTER is found, instead of MODULATION. Play Ex. 155.

From LITTLE PIANO BOOK. Permission for reprint granted by Elkan-Vogel Co., Inc., Philadelphia, Pa., copyright owners.

Find in piano literature examples of:
1. MODULATION (FROM WHAT KEY? To WHAT KEY?)
2. CHANGE OF TONAL CENTER

LESSON 90
Bridge, Transition, Episode

In order to move from one section to another, music of a *connective* nature is needed. This material, if short, is called a BRIDGE. Ordinarily, the BRIDGE is a measure or two of rhythm, scale, or arpeggio line. Play Ex. 156.

79

If the connective material is longer, it is called a TRANSITION. Play Ex. 157.

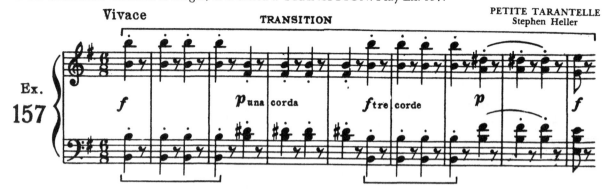

An example of a TRANSITION which modulates (from D♭ Major to V of A♭ Major). Play Ex. 158.

In a FUGUE or INVENTION the connective material is called EPISODE. The EPISODE may modulate or not, as needed. Play Ex. 159.

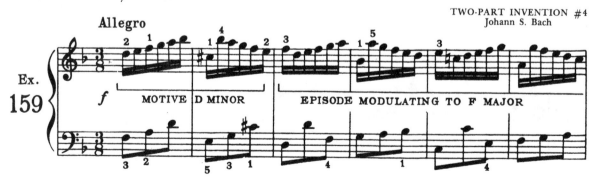

N3167

Find in piano literature examples of:
1. BRIDGE (A short connection)
2. TRANSITION (A longer connection)
3. EPISODE (The material between Motive or Subject statements in an Invention or Fugue)

LESSON 91
Codetta, Coda, Organ Point (Pedal Point)

A CODETTA (a short closing section) is often needed to round off a composition. Play Ex. 160.

If the closing section is longer and more elaborate, it is called a CODA. This type of ending is common in Sonatas and other large forms. Play Ex. 161.

81

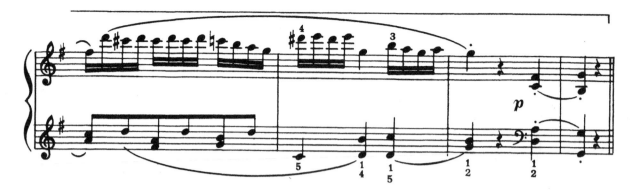

In contrapuntal music, a CODETTA is frequently an ORGAN POINT (PEDAL POINT), (a note held or repeated while the harmony changes in other parts). Play Ex. 162.

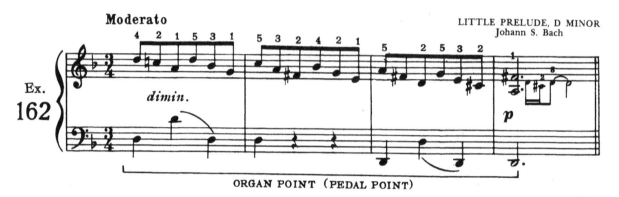

ORGAN POINT (PEDAL POINT)

Find in piano literature examples of:
1. CODETTA
2. CODA
3. ORGAN POINT (PEDAL POINT) used as closing material

LESSON 92
Review and Analysis

Find in the given music (Ex. 163):
1. MOTIVES (How many? How many measures in length?)
2. SEQUENCES (How many? Higher or lower?)
3. MODULATION (To what key?)
4. INVERSION OF MOTIVE
5. FRAGMENTS OF MOTIVE
6. SEMI-CADENCE
7. PERFECT AUTHENTIC CADENCE
8. CONTRASTING PHRASE CONSTRUCTION
9. HOW MANY PHRASES? HOW MANY MEASURES IN EACH PHRASE?
10. FORM AS A WHOLE

N3167

N3167

FOR COMPOSITIONAL ANALYSIS OF CONTEMPORARY MUSIC, SEE EXAMPLES BELOW.

MERRIMENT, FROM MIKROKOSMOS III, BELA BARTOK (Boosey-Hawkes)

Find:

    1. PENTATONIC SCALE
    2. INVERSION
    3. IMITATION A 5th BELOW
    4. INTRODUCTION AND CODETTA
    5. PHRASES (HOW MANY? HOW MANY MEASURES IN EACH PHRASE?)
    6. FORM AS A WHOLE

VARIATIONS FROM MIKROKOSMOS III

Find:

    1. 3-MEASURE PHRASES
    2. DORIAN MELODY (D TO D)
    3. IMITATION
    4. VARIATION (2 KINDS)
    5. SEQUENCE
    6. CHANGE OF REGISTER
    7. HOW MANY PHRASES? HOW MANY MEASURES IN EACH PHRASE?
    8. FORM AS A WHOLE

THE ABOVE REVIEW IS AN EXAMPLE OF THE ANALYTIC PROCESS WHICH SHOULD NOW
BE AN INTEGRAL PART OF THE STUDY OF ANY AND ALL PIANO MUSIC.

N3167

LANGUAGE OF THE PIANO

BIBLIOGRAPHY

COMPOSER	COMPOSITION	BOOK	EDITOR	PUBLISHER
ANDRE, A.	Sonatina, G	Easy Classics to Moderns	Agay	Consolidated
ANONYMOUS	Corranto, A Minor	Easy Elizabethans	Craxton	Oxford
ARNE, TH.	Gig	100 Best Short Classics, Bk. 1	Whitemore	Carl Fischer
ARNE, TH.	Minuet with Variations.	100 Best Short Classics, Bk. 1	Whitemore	Carl Fischer
ASTON, H.	Hornpype	Masters of the Keyboard	Willi Apel	Harvard
BACH, J. C.	Minuet to Dance	Sons of Bach	Hinrichsen	Schott
BACH, J. S.	Duet, A Minor	Road to Piano Artistry, Vol. 7	Scionti	Carl Fischer
BACH, J. S.	Fughetta, Dm.	Short Preludes and Fugues		Carl Fischer
BACH, J. S.	Gigue, A Major	From Bach to Beethoven, Vol. 2	Rehberg	Schott
BACH, J. S.	Little Prelude, C	Road to Piano Artistry, Vol. 2		Carl Fischer
BACH, J. S.	Little Prelude, C Minor	Short Preludes and Fugues		Carl Fischer
BACH, J. S.	Little Prelude, D Minor	Short Preludes and Fugues	Scionti	Carl Fischer
BACH, J. S.	Polonaise	Little Notebook for A. M. Bach		Kalmus
BACH, J. S.	Praeludium, C Major, #1	Well-Tempered Klavier, Bk. 1	G. Henle-Verlag	Carl Fischer
BACH, J. S.	Praeludium, C♯ Minor	Well-Tempered Klavier, Bk. 1	G. Henle-Verlag	Carl Fischer
BACH, J. S.	Sarabande	French Suite, D Minor	Busoni	Carl Fischer
BACH, J. S.	Three-Part Invention, #11	Road to Piano Artistry, Vol. 8	Scionti	Carl Fischer
BACH, J. S.	Two-Part Invention, #1	Road to Piano Artistry, Vol. 7	Scionti	Carl Fischer
BACH, J. S.	Two-Part Invention, #4	Two-Part Inventions	C. Czerny	Carl Fischer
BACH, J. S.	Two-Part Invention #2	Two-Part Inventions	C. Czerny	Carl Fischer
BACH, K. P. E.	Solfeggietto	Road to Piano Artistry, Vol. 6	Scionti	Carl Fischer
BARTOK, B.	Five-Finger Exercise	10 Easy Pieces	Agay	Leeds
BARTOK, B.	Game of Tag	85 Children's Pieces, Vol. 2		G. Schirmer
BARTOK, B.	Line and Point	Mikrokosmos, Vol. 2		Boosey-Hawkes
BARTOK, B.	Number 28	85 Children's Pieces, Vol. 1		G. Schirmer
BARTOK, B.	Number 34	Mikrokosmos, Vol. 1		Boosey-Hawkes
BARTOK, B.	Number 39	85 Children's Pieces, Vol. 1		G. Schirmer
BARTOK, B.	Slovakian Boys' Dance	10 Easy Pieces	Agay	Leeds
BARTOK, B.	Song of the Vagabond	85 Children's Pieces, Vol. 2		G. Schirmer
BARTOK, B.	Teasing	85 Children's Pieces, Vol. 2		G. Schirmer
BEETHOVEN, L.	Allemande, A Major	6 Allemandes		Omega
BEETHOVEN, L.	Bagatelle, C Minor	Klavierstucke, Bk. 1	G. Henle-Verlag	Carl Fischer
BEETHOVEN, L.	Bagatelle, D Major	Road to Piano Artistry, Vol. 3	Scionti	Carl Fischer
BEETHOVEN, L.	German Dance, #2	Piano Lit. 17th, 18th, 19th, Centuries		Summy
BEETHOVEN, L.	Menuet, C	Select Sonatinas, Vol. 1	Podolsky	Belwin
BEETHOVEN, L.	Minuetto from Sonata, Op. 49, #2	Road to Piano Artistry, Vol. 7	Scionti	Carl Fischer
BEETHOVEN, L.	Pastorale Dance	Pupils Classics—Portrait Albums First Series		
BEETHOVEN, L.	Scherzando	From Bach to Beethoven, Vol. 2	Rehberg	Arthur Schmidt
BEETHOVEN, L.	Scherzo from Sonata, Op. 28	Beethover, Sonatas, Vol. 2	Craxton-Tovey	Schott
				Ass. Board

LANGUAGE OF THE PIANO

BIBLIOGRAPHY

COMPOSER	COMPOSITION	BOOK	EDITOR	PUBLISHER
BEETHOVEN, L.	Waltz, F	Pupils Classics—Portrait Albums, First Series		Arthur Schmidt
BLOCH, E.	Lullaby	Enfantines		Carl Fischer
BULL, J.	The King's Hunting Jigg	Old Masters of 16th, 17th, 18 Centuries	Herrmann	Kalmus
BUTTSTEDT, J.	Minuet, F	Easy Comp. from Three Centuries	Herrmann	Kalmus
BYRD, WM.	A Gigge	Easy Elizabethans	Craxton	Oxford
BYRD, WM.	Callino Casturami	Easy Elizabethans	Craxton	Oxford
CASELLA, A.	Minuetto	11 Children's Pieces		Associated
CHOPIN, F.	Mazurka, Op. 7, #2	Mazurkas	I. Friedman	Carl Fischer
CHOPIN, F.	Mazurka, Op. 30, #2	Mazurkas	I. Friedman	Carl Fischer
CHOPIN, F.	Mazurka, Op. 41, #1	Mazurkas	I. Friedman	Carl Fischer
CHOPIN, F.	Nocturne, Op. 37, #1	Nocturnes	Pinter	Carl Fischer
CHOPIN, F.	Prelude, B Minor	Preludes	Eckstein	Carl Fischer
CIMAROSA, D.	Sonata, #11	32 Sonatas	Boghen. Eschig	Associated
CIMAROSA, D.	Sonata, #17	32 Sonatas	Boghen. Eschig	Associated
CZERNY, C.	Sonatina, Op. 792	Select Sonatinas, Vol. 1	Podolsky	Belwin
CZERNY, C.	Study #12	Selected Studies, Vol. 994		G. Schirmer
DAQUIN, LOUIS	Tambourin	Easy Comp. From 3 Centuries	Herrmann	Kalmus
DIABELLI, A.	Sonatina, F Major	Select Sonatinas, Vol. 1	Podolsky	Belwin
FARNABY, G.	A Toye	Recital Repertoire, Vol. 1	Podolsky	Belwin
FRANCK, C.	Puppet's Complaint	Easy Classics to Moderns	Agay	Consolidated
FREED, I.	With Trumpets and Drums	Masters of Our Day		Carl Fischer
GALUPPI, B.	Gigue from Sonata, D	Classic Sonatas	Podolsky	Carl Fischer
GREENE, M.	Allemande	Ayres and Dances	F. Moore	Paterson's
GRETCHANINOFF, A.	Nurse's Tale, Op. 109, #9	A Child's Day	Schott	Associated
GURLITT, C.	Study #18	School of Velocity, Op. 141		G. Schirmer
HANDEL, G. F.	Courante, F	100 Best Short Classics, Vol. 2	Whitemore	Carl Fischer
HANDEL, G. F.	Little Fugue, #1	6 Easy Fugues	Marion Bauer	Axelrod
HANDEL, G. F.	Little Fugue, #5	6 Easy Fugues	Marion Bauer	Axelrod
HANDEL, G. F.	Passacaglia	7th Suite, G Minor	B. Fisk	Schroeder-Gunther
HASSE, J. A.	Adagio from Sonata, D Minor	Classic Sonatas	Podolsky	Carl Fischer
HASSLER, J.	Allegro, Little Suite #3	Select Sonatinas, Bk. 1	Podolsky	Belwin
HASSLER, J.	Andante, Little Suite #2	Select Sonatinas, Bk. 1	Podolsky	Belwin
HASSLER, J.	Menuetto, Little Suite #1	Select Sonatinas, Bk. 1	Podolsky.	Belwin
HAYDN, FRANZ J.	Andantino	From Bach to Beethoven, Vol. 2	Rehberg	Schott
HAYDN, FRANZ J.	Andante Grazioso	Early Classics, Bk. 2	Mirovitch	G. Schirmer
HAYDN, FRANZ J.	German Dance, #4	Easy Classics to Moderns	Agay	Consolidated
HAYDN, FRANZ J.	Theme, from Sonata, G Major	Master Series		G. Schirmer
HELLER, ST.	At the Spinning Wheel	25 Melodious Studies	E. Hughes	Carl Fischer

COMPOSER	COMPOSITION	BOOK	EDITOR	PUBLISHER
HELLER, ST.	Berceuse	100 Best Short Classics, Vol. 1	Whitemore	Carl Fischer
HELLER, ST.	Coquetry, Op. 47, #3	Road to Piano Artistry, Vol. 1	Scionti	Carl Fischer
HELLER, ST.	Curious Story	Road to Piano Artistry, Vol. 3	Scionti	Carl Fischer
HELLER, ST.	Petite Tarantelle	Road to Piano Artistry, Vol. 4	Scionti	Carl Fischer
HELLER, ST.	Triumph (Allamarcia)	25 Studies for Rhythm and Expression	Gahm	Carl Fischer
ILJINSKY, A.	Berceuse, Op. 13, #7	Masterpieces of Piano Music	Wier	Carl Fischer
KABALEVSKY, D.	A Little Song	15 Children's Pieces, Op. 27, Bk. 1	Mirovitch	Leeds
KABALEVSKY, D.	A Short Story	15 Children's Pieces, Op. 27, Bk. 1	Mirovitch	Leeds
KABALEVSKY, D.	Dance on the Lawn	15 Children's Pieces, Op. 27, Bk. 1	Mirovitch	Leeds
KABALEVSKY, D.	Etude	15 Children's Pieces, Op. 27, Bk. 1	Mirovitch	Leeds
KABALEVSKY, D.	Toccatina	15 Children's Pieces, Op. 27, Bk. 1	Mirovitch	Leeds
KIRNBERGER, J.	Invention and Little Fugue	Intro. to Piano Classics, Vol. 1	Mirovitch	G. Schirmer
KUHLAU, F.	Vivace, Sonatina, Op. 55, #1	Road to Piano Artistry, Vol. 2	Scionti	Carl Fischer
LIADOW, A.	Mazurka, Rustique, Op. 15, #1	Medieval Modes	Richardson	H. W. Gray
LOEILLY (LOEILLET), J.	Cibel	Contemporaries of Purcell	Herrmann	Hinrichsen
LOEILLY (LOEILLET), J.	Gigue, G Minor			
MARPURG, F.	Menuet	Easy Comp. from 3 Centuries	A. Spencer	Summy
MILHAUD, D.	Dawn	Une Journee	Herrmann	Kalmus
MILHAUD, D.	Touches Blanches	Masters of Our Day		Mercury
MILHAUD, D.	Touches Noires	Masters of Our Day		Carl Fischer
MENDELSSOHN, F.	Song Without Words, #9	Songs Without Words	Goetschius	Carl Fischer
MENDELSSOHN, F.	Song Without Words, #14	Songs Without Words	Goetschius	Ditson
MONN, G. M.	Allegretto	Easy Comp. From 3 Centuries	Herrmann	Ditson
MOORE, DOUGLAS	Fiddlin' Joe	Masters of Our Day		Kalmus
MOORE, DOUGLAS	Grievin' Annie	Masters of Our Day		Carl Fischer
MOORE, JOHN	It's A Bright Morning	Work and Play		Carl Fischer
MOSKOWSKI, M.	Pantomime, Op. 77, #8			Boston
MOZART, L. W.	Burleske	Easy Comp. From 3 Centuries	Herrmann	G. Schirmer
MOZART, L. W.	Fantasia	Piano Music Notebook		Kalmus
MOZART, L. W.	Musette, Little Suite #3	Select Sonatinas, Vol. 1	Podolsky	Omega
MOZART, L. W.	Polonaise, Suite #4	Leopold Mozart's Little Piano Book		Belwin
MOZART, L. W.	Sarabande	Airs and Dances	H. Kreutzer	Kalmus
MOZART, W. A.	Ah, Vous Dirai-Je	Variations	Siloti	Boston
MOZART, W. A.	Allegro, Salzburg	Select Pieces, Bk. 1	Herrmann	Carl Fischer
MOZART, W. A.	Andante from Sonata K545	Sonatas, Vol. 2		Peters
MOZART, W. A.	Andantino, K236	Intro. to Piano Classics, Bk. 1	G. Henle-Verlag	Carl Fischer
MOZART, W. A.	Menuetto, Viennese Sonatina #6	6 Viennese Sonatinas	Mirovitch	G. Schirmer
MOZART, W. A.	Minuet, F	100 Best Short Classics, Vol. 1	W. Rehberg	Associated
MOZART, W. A.	Minuetto, Viennese Sonatina #2	Road to Piano Artistry, Vol. 3	Whitemore	Carl Fischer
			Scionti	Carl Fischer

LANGUAGE OF THE PIANO

BIBLIOGRAPHY

COMPOSER	COMPOSITION	BOOK	EDITOR	PUBLISHER
MOZART, W. A.	Minuet and Trio	Piano Lit. 17th, 18th, 19th Centuries	Clarke	Summy
MOZART, W. A.	Presto, Sonata G (K283)	Klavier Sonaten, Bk. 1	G. Henle-Verlag	Carl Fischer
MOZART, W. A.	Rondoletto	First Year Classics	Krentzlin	Arthur Schmidt
MOZART, W. A.	Sonata, K283	Klaviersonaten, Bk. 1	G. Henle-Verlag	Carl Fischer
MOZART, W. A.	Waltz—3 Waltzes	100 Best Short Classics, Vol. 1	Whitemore	Carl Fischer
PARADISI, P.	Vivace from Sonata in D	Classic Sonatas	Podolsky	Carl Fischer
PERSICHETTI, V.	Dialogue	Little Piano Book		Elkan-Vogel
PERSICHETTI, V.	Prologue	Little Piano Book		Elkan-Vogel
PERSICHETTI, V.	Statement	Little Piano Book		Elkan-Vogel
PROKOFIEFF, S.	Fairy-Tale, Op. 65, #3	Music for Children	Wolman	Leeds
PURCELL, H.	Prelude	Purcell-Arne Album		Boston
REBIKOV, V.	Mazurka, Op. 8, #9			Carl Fischer
REBIKOV, V.	Strolling Musicians, Op. 31			G. Schirmer
REINHOLD, H.	Nachtstuck	Miniatures	Oesterle	G. Schirmer
REINHOLD, H.	Serenade	Miniatures	Oesterle	G. Schirmer
RIEGGER, W.	Chromatics	New and Old		Boosey-Hawkes
SCARLATTI, A.	Air from Toccata	Early Italian Piano Music	Shaw	J. Fischer
SCARLATTI, A.	Minuetto	Early Italian Piano Music	Shaw	J. Fischer
SCARLATTI, D.	Sonate #3	25 Sonatas	Sauer	Peters
SCHUBERT, F.	Allegretto, From Minuet, F	Easy Classics to Moderns	Agay	Consolidated
SCHUBERT, F.	Ecossaise, G	Intro. to Piano Classics, Bk. 2	Mirovitch	G. Schirmer
SCHUBERT, F.	Impromptu, Op. 90, #4	Schubert Album	Gallico	Ed. Marks
SCHUBERT, F.	Impromptu, Ab, Op. 142, #2	Schubert Album	Gallico	Ed. Marks
SCHUBERT, F.	Waltz, Ab	Old Tunes for Young Pianists, Bk. 4	Prahl	Carl Fischer
SCHUMANN, R.	Echoes from the Theatre	Album for the Young	Eckstein	Carl Fischer
SCHUMANN, R.	First Loss	Album for the Young	Eckstein	Carl Fischer
SCHUMANN, R.	Important Event	Scenes from Childhood	Eckstein	Carl Fischer
SCHUMANN, R.	Siciliano	Album for the Young	Eckstein	Carl Fischer
SCHUMANN, R.	Soldiers March	Album for the Young	Eckstein	Carl Fischer
SHOSTAKOVITCH, D.	A Happy Fairy Tale	6 Children's Pieces	Wolman	Leeds
SHOSTAKOVITCH, D.	The Mechanical Doll	6 Children's Pieces	Wolman	Leeds
STOLTZE, R.	Traffic Dance			Composers Press
SWEELINK, J. P.	Pavana Hispanica	17th Century Masters	Herrmann	International
TANSMAN, A.	The Young Swing Pianist	Pour Les Enfants, Bk. 2	Eschig	Associated
TELEMAN, G.	Minuet in G	Easy Comp. From 3 Centuries	Herrmann	Kalmus
TCHAIKOWSKY, P.	Mazurka, Op. 39, #10	Road to Piano Artistry, Vol. 2	Scionti	Carl Fischer
TCHAIKOWSKY, P.	The Sick Doll	Album for the Young, Op. 39	Eckstein	Carl Fischer
TURINA, J.	Fiesta	Miniatures		Associated
WITTE, CH.	Minuet, C	Easy Comp. From 3 Centuries	Herrmann	Kalmus